A HEART
TO LISTEN

Text copyright © Michael Mitton 2004
The author asserts the moral right
to be identified as the author of this work

Published by
The Bible Reading Fellowship
First Floor, Elsfield Hall
15–17 Elsfield Way, Oxford OX2 8FG

ISBN 1 84101 269 6

First published 2004
10 9 8 7 6 5 4 3 2 1
All rights reserved

Acknowledgments
Unless otherwise stated, scripture quotations are taken from The New Revised Standard
Version of the Bible, Anglicized Edition, copyright © 1989, 1995 by the Division of Christian
Education of the National Council of the Churches of Christ in the USA, and are used by
permission. All rights reserved.

Scripture quotations taken from the Holy Bible, New International Version, copyright © 1973,
1978, 1984 by International Bible Society, are used by permission of Hodder & Stoughton
Limited. All rights reserved. 'NIV' is a registered trademark of International Bible Society.
UK trademark number 1448790.

Scripture quotations from THE MESSAGE. Copyright © by Eugene H. Peterson 1993, 1994,
1995. Used by permission of NavPress Publishing Group.

Scripture quotations from the Good News Bible published by The Bible Societies/HarperCollins
Publishers are copyright © 1966, 1971, 1976, 1992 American Bible Society.

A catalogue record for this book is available from the British Library

Printed and bound in Singapore by Craft Print International Ltd

A HEART TO LISTEN

BECOMING A LISTENING PERSON
IN A NOISY WORLD

Michael Mitton

To Anne Long
Pastor, Pioneer and Prophet

PREFACE

This book was written during my last months of working with the Acorn Christian Foundation. I would like to record my thanks to the Trustees and staff of Acorn who allowed me space to write it. I am particularly grateful to Russ Parker, who for six years has been both my very dear friend and a wonderful colleague. I asked him to write the foreword because of both these important roles that he has played in my life. As a colleague, he has watched my deepening passion for the ministry of listening. Not only has he watched it, he has encouraged it and contributed to it. As Director of Acorn, a healing ministry, he affirms that increasingly close marriage of the ministries of healing and listening. As a friend, he knows well my own personal story and the journeys that I have travelled, a number of which have shaped this book.

I also want to thank the Christian Listeners staff team. One of the hardest parts of leaving Acorn, for me, has been leaving this remarkable team. Each member is not only utterly dedicated to their work but they demonstrate so clearly in their lives a very high quality of listening. I have been inspired by each one of them more than I can say, and my life feels so much deeper and richer as a consequence. So thank you Anne, Ffion, Heather, Joy, Lynne, Marianne, Marie, Mary, Pat, Peter, Robin, Ruth, Sue, and Tricia.

Finally, I have dedicated this book to Anne Long. It was Anne who got me started on this road, and for the last few years I have had the privilege of being entrusted with the work she began in Acorn. I believe that Anne's ministry to the Church of all denominations has been truly prophetic. With steadfastness of vision, she has proclaimed with clarity, conviction and practical application the vital importance of this ministry of listening. There are thousands who owe so much to Anne, either directly or through those she has trained. This book will not do justice to the quality of her listening training and care, but I hope it will in some measure be a signal to her, to let her know how grateful so many of us are.

CONTENTS

FOREWORD

I will keep this brief because I want you to join Michael on his listening journey, which is richly rewarding to read. Threaded through his book is a deeply ingrained passion and conviction about the utter necessity for us to become listeners above and before all other things. All the prayers we offer to God are on the correct assumption that he is listening closely to what we are saying. Jesus himself told us that everything he did was out of his listening and observation of what he saw his Father doing. We live in a world clamouring for our attention and this is best conveyed by our listening rather than by our proclamations. It was Michael who powerfully reminded me that, out of all the therapies we give to others, listening is the only one that does no harm or damage to the other.

This book invites you to take a journey of discovery about what lies at the heart of listening, and in so doing you will, with me, realize how difficult and how rewarding becoming an accurate listener really is. Michael is my best friend as well as being a colleague on the Acorn staff for the last six years. I think all of us would want to put on record that he has shown himself to be a man who listens to his team in such a way as to bring the best out of them and for them. He listened to me during times of great turmoil in my life and I am the better for it.

I am greatly excited about this book. Read it and be blessed!

Russ Parker

Chapter 1

TO AWAKEN THE HEART

Seldom is the human spirit
Given the honour of the listening ear;
But the gift of God
Is to awaken the heart.

In 1996, on a warm June evening in a pub in central London, I was enjoying a drink with two good friends. One was Russ Parker, whom I have known and loved as a great friend for many years, and the other was Charles Longbottom, whom I had been getting to know through a joint project in which we were involved. At the time, I was Director of Anglican Renewal Ministries, Russ was the Director of the Acorn Christian Foundation, and Charles was the Chairman of Acorn. In the course of the conversation I asked Charles his opinion about what I should do after my time with ARM had come to an end. Without hesitation, and much to my surprise, he said, 'Join the staff of Acorn and take on the work of Christian Listeners after Anne Long retires.'

I travelled home on the train, my mind buzzing with many conflicting thoughts. I was happy in my work with ARM and loved the new openings that it was giving me, especially contacts I was beginning to make with equivalent organizations in different parts of the world. I had not long returned from wonderful visits to East Africa and India, and my heart had been deeply stirred by such immediate contacts with the developing world. Furthermore, renewal was at an exciting stage and important developments for renewal were taking place in the Anglican communion. In fact, I thought of many good reasons not to leave my current work. But the invitation to consider the work with Acorn did not go away, and the next stage was to meet with Anne Long, who was then the National Coordinator of Christian Listeners.

I first met Anne 20 years ago, when I began a two-year course at St John's College, Nottingham. I still feel full of gratitude to God for the two very formative years I spent there, which proved to be an excellent foundation for my ministry as an Anglican priest. During the mid 1970s, St Johns was fully engaged in charismatic renewal, and had that ability both to experience the renewal and to reflect on it critically and theologically. Also, one of the effects of the renewal in the 1970s was to free evangelicals to explore beyond the rather rigid spiritual boundaries that had hitherto existed. Anne Long was particularly helpful in this regard. With clearly held evangelical convictions, she nonetheless taught us how to explore the worlds of catholic spirituality as well as the world of 'secular' counselling and therapy. These were two new directions for me (though guideposts for them have always been there in my heart), and Anne taught me how to travel down both of these roads. They have been roads of wonderful discovery for me throughout my ministry.

As I reflect on the training I received at St Johns, I am convinced that what has helped me more than anything has been the listening and counselling training that Anne offered. Not only this but she also led a personal growth group that lasted for a year. This group of students, led by Anne, met regularly, and in the increasingly safe context of the group we were invited to explore areas of personal growth. I am in no doubt at all that the healing that took place within that group, and the insights I gained from the counselling training, are the main reason why I have not sustained serious emotional injury from the many pressures that assail clergy.

I learned much from Anne Long, and from Dr Frank Lake, who was a regular visitor to St John's. Both stressed the importance of listening as a foundation not only to counselling but to all human growth. After I left St Johns and became a parish priest, I continued my connection with the world of counselling and listening by being a tutor on the St John's Extension Studies Pastoral Counselling courses. I eventually gave this up in 1989 when I became Director of Anglican Renewal Ministries. In this job I was less directly involved pastorally with people, though I regularly needed to offer a listening ear. Often this was to clergy attending our conferences who were facing struggles in their parish. At other times, good listening was necessary in more diplomatic situations, with people who were quite opposed to charismatic renewal, often because they had been hurt by it. I frequently had cause to feel grateful for my listening and counselling training.

The invitation to join the staff of Acorn was one that would take me back into the world of pastoral care. I was far from certain that I wanted to return to this world, however, so I entered a time of listening to God, to myself and to others to discern the way forward, and over a period of time it became clear that God was directing me in this way. Thus it was that I found myself at a commissioning service in Derby Cathedral on 1 October 1997, beginning my new journey with Acorn.

A JOURNEY OF DISCOVERY

The past six years have been a journey of discovery for me. To be honest, when I first started with Acorn and people asked me what I did, I never thought it sounded very impressive to say, 'I do listening training.' It felt so much less dynamic than saying, 'I am encouraging renewal in the church.' I had no dramatic stories of revival to offer, no articles to write with thrilling headlines. I found myself being a little apologetic, and I noticed that the other person's response would often be a kindly nod, which I interpreted along the lines of 'Well, I suppose somebody's got to do it.' And yes, I would think, somebody has got to do it. There are precious few listeners around.

I had inherited a wonderful regional team of staff from Anne Long, and excellent resources, and it has always felt a great privilege to offer this listening training. At staff meetings I would see one of the staff light up as they told a story of a training seminar and the often dramatic impact of listening training. I felt very privileged to be part of this, but I think, in all honesty, it had not reached that place in my heart where I hold my deepest convictions. As I listened to those deepest places of my heart, I kept on discovering a longing for the poor and the marginalized, and for those outside the Church who have never heard that there is a healing God who loves them with eternal love. Once or twice I travelled off to do a talk on listening somewhere, and found myself inwardly agonizing that all I was doing was offering more resources for middle-class Christians who already had more than they needed.

These uncomfortable feelings ebbed and flowed, and the time came for me to consider renewing my contract with Acorn or moving on. I was coming to the conclusion that it was right for me to consider moving on to another work, one that would be driven by the callings from deep within my inner self. Then I visited South Africa.

In the early 1990s, Archbishop Desmond Tutu contacted Anne Long to ask if she would come to South Africa and introduce listening training to the Centre for Christian Spirituality that he was developing in Cape Town. The upshot of this was that several teams of Christian Listeners have visited not only Cape Town but other parts of South Africa during the last few years, and there are now centres established in the Western Cape, Eastern Cape, Gauteng, and KwaZulu Natal. I was asked to visit the emerging teams to foster the link of Acorn's work in the UK and South Africa. Thus it was, on a dark January day in 2001, that I found myself packing my suitcase in preparation for my first long-haul journey for many years.

On the night before I left, my wife Julia woke up and thought, 'It's 3.14am.' She turned over and looked at her bedside clock and, sure enough, it was 3.14am, and she found herself thinking, 'Exactly right.' It was at this point that she sensed God was speaking to her, as he has often done in the quietness of the night. She felt God was saying that it was exactly right that I should be visiting South Africa at this time. She wanted to get up but found that it was a great struggle. She managed it, however, and felt God then speaking to her about the struggle we have in hearing how important listening is to him. She wrote down what she sensed God saying to her and gave it to me before I departed. I read it again as the huge jet heaved me up into a damp January sky and over the south of England, then France, the Mediterranean and on the long, long flight over the vast lands of Africa. As I pondered all this, I felt somewhat convicted that I had overlooked the obvious. The reason I was doing this listening work was not because it happened to be a job that became available at the right time. It began to dawn on me that God had actually led me into a ministry that was much more to do with the depths within my own heart than I had realized. Not only this, but I was beginning to appreciate just how important this listening ministry is in the work of the kingdom of God.

The climate in Cape Town could not have been more different from the one I left in London. Suddenly it was summer! One of the Christian Listener tutors in Cape Town met me and drove me away from the airport. We almost immediately passed one of the communities called 'informal settlements'. These are large communities of black folk who live in houses that are little more than huts made out of corrugated iron. I clearly remembered these communities from when I last visited South Africa, before the elections, when I visited a number and had the privilege of preaching in the churches and being entertained in the homes. As we drove past them I suddenly felt gripped by strong emotions and longed to visit these places of poverty. Previous encounters with these communities had had a healing effect in my soul, in that they had shown me about qualities of life that are all-too-often lost in our materialist Western world.

Not long after driving past this community, I met up with a very good friend, Bishop Eric Pike, and his wife Joyce. Eric had recently retired as the bishop of Port Elizabeth and he and Joyce now live in Cape Town. It was Bishop Eric who, on a previous visit to South Africa in 1993, had taken me to a Mothers' Union meeting in the township of New Brighton. It was my first visit to a township, and one that I shall always cherish. In the midst of the anxiety and violence of that pre-election era, here was an oasis of hope. Here there was singing that somehow gathered up the voice of a suffering people and expressed it harmoniously in praise and supplication to God. Here I witnessed Bishop Eric's love for the black community as he spoke to them fluently in their language of Xhosa. Eric was one to lead with his ears, as it were, and he dared to listen to the deep pains of the people of his diocese. It was therefore good for me to be with him that afternoon, as he shared his understanding of the situation in his beloved country.

Eric then drove me to my next meeting, taking the coastal route, and at one point passed a beach full of happy bathers. 'Do you see that beach?' he said. 'This has always been a beach that coloured folk love to use. But during apartheid, they were forbidden to use their beach. Can you imagine that?' he said, swallowing back a pain familiar to those white South Africans who have always loved the black and coloured communities. 'But now look—they can swim there again. It is so wonderful to see!' Once again I felt honoured to be with one of the many white people who suffered so deeply during the years of apartheid, and whose acts of prayer and protest contributed to the birthing of this rainbow nation, a rainbow formed by the love of God shining through many tears. It soon became clear to me that the tears are still evident in South Africa and that there are many pains in all sections of the community that need the warm rays of the love of God expressed through a listening ear.

That evening, I met with the group of trained Christian Listeners at the Centre for Spirituality in Cape Town. A man called Ed Coombe led the meeting. Like Bishop Eric, he was one of those who had keenly felt the pains of apartheid, and the wounds were still evident in his soul. But all this had made him a man of deep compassion. He opened the meeting with devotions based on the set reading for the day in the South African Anglican lectionary, which was the call of Matthew. He then offered a few comments on this reading, in which he urged us to see how we could take our listening training to the 'Matthews' of this world—the outsiders and the marginalized. He quoted from John Wesley, who once said, 'Go not only to those who need you, but to those who need you most.'

Only a few times in my life have I felt the word of the Lord come to me with such directness that it seemed like the experience described by the writer to the Hebrews—as 'sharper than any two-edged sword, piercing until it divides soul from spirit, joints from marrow' (Hebrews 4:12). This time was one of them. I knew that even if nothing else significant were to happen, it was worth my travelling all the way to Cape Town to collect this word from the Lord. Without any doubt, I knew in my spirit that this was God saying to me, 'Go now with this listening gift not only to those who need you, but to those who need you most.' Put alongside the word Julia had heard from God two nights before, I was left in no doubt that I was being called back into Acorn, and the specific calling was not only to take this gift of listening to those who need us, but particularly to seek out 'those who need us most'.

I was impressed by all the Christian Listeners I met in South Africa, and there was no question that in their hearts they also shared the conviction that their listening training was to be taken to those who need us most. But before my visit came to an end, I was to experience another moment of listening to God that was to make a great impression on me.

KWAZULU NATAL

The last stop on my journey in South Africa was to the province of KwaZulu Natal. The leaders of the Christian Listening work here are Jim and Heather Johnston, who run the Beth Shalam Retreat Centre situated in the hills that overlook Pietermartizburg. Jim and Heather originally hail from Northern Ireland, but have lived in South Africa for most of their lives and have a deep love for the people they serve. They have grown particularly close to the Zulu peoples in the KwaZulu Natal Midlands, an area that has been severely ravaged by HIV/AIDS. Jim and Heather have taken the listening training to this community, and have been part of a team producing a listening course for those caring for people living with AIDS. The course is called 'Listening to pain and hope'.

Thus it was, on a Friday morning in January, that they drove me out of fogbound Pietermartizburg, north to the majestic Drakensburg mountains and on to the vast plains that hold a multitude of rural communities, all of whom have been buffeted by this brutal disease. We arrived in the small town of Bergville, where we met Phumzile Ndlovu, the Co-ordinator of World Vision's Child Survival Project and the Home-Based Care Programme for HIV/AIDS sufferers.

The home-based project started in 1999 and trains volunteers from the local communities to visit those who are terminally ill and to offer support to the families before and after the death. In the Bergville region there are currently 80 visitors, mostly women. Phumzile introduced us to three of the volunteer home-based carers who shared their stories. Between them they have cared for 57 patients, all of whom have died.

One of these visitors told us about her work.

I go to a household where there is a terminal patient. Sometimes the health worker tells me the person has AIDS and tells me how to look after this person. When I go to the household, I don't stay there, but I request to see a family member and train them to look after the patient. All family members need to be talked to. If the person has a wound, I teach them how to wash and dress the wound. I teach the family that they must give that person love. I also encourage them to eat nutritious food. Sometimes the terminally ill patient is the breadwinner and so there is no food in the home. Then I encourage the family to do the small gardens, but the trouble is that they have not enough money to buy the seed. In some situations, when there is no money for seed, I take the difficult decision of taking money from my family and buy spinach seed for this family. Some of my patients don't have faith. We have some Bibles to give out, so I offer it to them and say, 'Do you know this book?' I leave it with them, and return the following day, and say, 'This book contains stories that will give you eternal life.' The Bible stories show the way to faith and hope—the promise of eternal life even after death. If the person is a parent and we know they are going to die, we talk with them about who will care for the children.

We are spending much time with the orphans—we sympathize with them and we help them to face their situation. All the supervisors meet together and we have corporate supervision and share what's on our heart. It is very painful—the person whom you have cared for who dies is part of your body. When you go to the altar by yourself, you pour your heart out to God and it helps you to face the truth that we are all going to die one day. Families often continue friendship with the caregiver.

I found myself feeling intensely moved as I listened to these women tell their stories of providing such generous care to those stricken with AIDS. I was also thrilled to hear them speak of how much the listening training was helping them. Such is the enthusiasm for listening training and the 'Listening to pain and hope' course that, at the time of writing, I have heard that 700 of these home-based carers are receiving listening training. For me, this was a moment of revelation, of transition—a movement from seeing listening training as simply helpful to seeing it as a vital Christ-like gift to offer to those who need it most.

I returned to the retreat centre with Jim and Heather feeling rather stunned. That evening I was on my own and suddenly felt the Lord very close to me. So I got out my laptop and started to write what was in my heart. I found myself writing prophetically—I was not sure whether it was from God or from a deep and hitherto unheard place in my own heart. I did not mind too much which it was, because it was important to listen to both voices. Both had something important to say. Among the thoughts that came to me that evening was the following:

Why do I need people to listen?
Why do I need an army of listeners?
Because my house has been a rebellious house
The proud speak and speak and feel they have the answers...

The earth is sick because few have listened to it.
The church is sick because people speak when they should listen.
My poor are sick because people speak about them
but will not listen to them.

Why do I need my people to listen?
Because when you listen you meet me in my glory.
You will encounter me in such a way as to transform nations.
You humble yourself to become the meek who inherit the earth.
You relinquish your power.
You let go of what you want to say,
and instead, you wait as you listen,
and then you speak to what you hear,
and that word will be wisdom.
My world suffers because of lack of wisdom;
wisdom is not gained by talking but by listening.
The fool speaks and plans and fills all silences.
The wise one is prepared to look foolish by remaining silent
until they hear a word from the Lord.
This incessant talking has cut my people off from the living word.

When the poor are listened to,
they start to believe that they are being noticed.
I am among the poor;
you hear my word amongst them,
and then you release my word to the world,
and when my word is released my world will find healing.

GOD'S HEART FOR LISTENING

Given that I was listening to what was probably a mixture of my own heart and the heart of God, nonetheless I felt that within it I heard very clearly God's longing that we might learn to listen better.

This was confirmed for me on my return to England. I contacted Anne Long, as I wanted to check out with her my experiences in South Africa and to check them against the vision God had originally given her for Christian Listeners. When I met with her, she told me that she had been listening to God through reading the Psalms in Eugene Petersen's THE MESSAGE, and the set Psalms for the day I met with her were Psalms 81 and 95. She had been particularly struck by these passages:

> *But my people didn't listen, Israel paid no attention;*
> *So I let go of the reins and told them, 'Run! Do it your own way!'*
> *Oh dear people will you listen to me now?*
> *Israel, will you follow my map?*
>
> PSALM 81

> *Drop everything and listen, listen as he speaks:*
> *Don't turn a deaf ear as in the Bitter Uprising,*
> *As on the day of the Wilderness Test,*
> *when your ancestors turned and put me to the test.*
> *For forty years they watched me at work among them,*
> *as over and over they tried my patience.*
> *And I was provoked—oh, was I provoked!*
> *'Can't they keep their minds on God for five minutes?*
> *Do they simply refuse to walk down my road?'*
> *Exasperated, I exploded,*
> *'They'll never get where they're headed,*
> *never be able to sit down and rest.'*
>
> PSALM 95

We both felt we heard very clearly in these modern translations of ancient words the utter exasperation of God, who longs that we might be a listening people. We also heard the sad consequences of our stubborn failure to listen. Very simply, we lose our way.

In my time of listening to God and to my own heart after my day in Bergville, I was fascinated to hear of the connection between listening and 'transforming nations'. I felt rather sceptical about this: was it a grandiose part of me getting rather carried away? But then, a couple of months after returning, I received an e-mail from Joanna Zeiner, a Christian Listener tutor in KZN who had been advertising a Christian Listening seminar in Natal Seminary. She advertised the seminar using our Acorn mission statement: 'Bringing the healing of Jesus Christ to a broken world'. A student from Burundi, Freddy Tuyezere, saw the poster and wrote to her: 'When you say, "bringing the healing of Jesus Christ to a broken world", I just see my nation destroyed by wars and divisions. People are so discouraged there. Can you please allow me to start listening, and then help peace to come to my lovely country.'

I have always been impressed with the way African people are able to see things holistically. Typically, the African Freddy had seen that there was a link between listening and the healing of a nation. When people start to listen to one another, the mechanism for reconciliation is put into place and this is hugely significant for a nation torn apart by conflict.

I am writing this book in my final weeks with Acorn. It is thrilling for me to see that much of the vision that I have described in these first pages of the book is now finding an outworking in Acorn's listening ministry. The staff are working harder than ever to share listening training with many people. Moreover, Acorn has set up a Priority Area Listening ministry, where they are deliberately seeking out those parts of our society that need the ministry most, and equipping churches to set up listening projects in their communities to enable hurting and broken people to tell their stories and find pathways of healing. I also leave at a time when the resources of Acorn are becoming increasingly available to the poor of the developing world, especially those afflicted with HIV/AIDS. I have no doubt that God will use this gift to touch those lives that are so precious to him.

For me, these six years with Acorn have been a time of a change of heart. I feel that God has awoken my heart to the realization that listening is not simply a pastoral tool for people who rather like counselling-related activities. It is fundamental to our humanity, and crucial for the way we treat each other. I know I have deeply changed, and for the rest of my life I shall value listening as one of the most healing gifts that we can possess.

This is not going to be an erudite book full of footnotes to impress you! Neither is it a handbook on how to listen. If you would like something more practical, then I refer you to Anne Long's excellent book called *Listening* (DLT, 1990) and the Acorn Christian Listener courses, which are listed in an appendix at the end. This book is more of an exploration of why listening is an important gift, and how it is a gift that is so necessary for today's culture.

When I wrote my book on the healing ministry, *Wild Beasts and Angels*,[1] I decided to risk including a narrative tale that ran through the chapters and served as a parable. I had so many positive comments about this story that I have decided to do the same with this book. The aim of the narrative is simply to convey the main theme of the chapter in the context of a short story, to help in the process of reflecting on the theme. It is an entirely fictional story based in Africa. It could have been set anywhere in the developing world but, because of my experience in South Africa, it felt most natural to root my story there. The aim of writing this story is to say much the same thing as the main text, but in a different way. My prayer is that as you read the pages of this book, both the main text and the story, you will receive that gift of God that awakens both the mind and the heart.

THE SPEAKER (I)

The conference was well organized—very well organized. There were delegates from several countries. There was a government minister who sat at the front, although he kept having to go out to speak on his mobile phone. Everyone had very smart-looking name badges. And of course there was the Speaker—a very intelligent man who was very well dressed, very knowledgeable and used his PowerPoint presentation very well indeed. Nice use of colours, if rather too many words.

Nkani had never seen PowerPoint before. He liked it. He liked the pie charts best—something about them made him want to giggle. Looked at in a certain way, they seemed like funny faces, and some humour was worth a lot in this rather boring conference. Not that the subject was boring—just the way the Speaker addressed it. Actually, Nkani had never been to a conference like this before. It was the first time he had ever travelled out of his village, so everything was new and strange. He had been invited and sponsored, and when he had been told that he had been selected to travel to England for this conference, he felt as if someone had given him one of the stars from the sky. 'Your English is so good,' he was told. And they were right; it was—which meant that he could understand most of what the people on the platform were saying.

'I think I speak for us all,' said a man in a pinstriped suit next to the Speaker, 'when I say that we shall always be indebted to our speaker today. His knowledge about AIDS is truly impressive, and the thesis he has presented to us this afternoon will give us food for thought for a very long time to come. I'm pleased to say that he can stay with us for a few more minutes before he leaves to catch the evening flight to Edinburgh, where he is speaking at another high-level conference tomorrow. So this gives us a chance for some questions. Could I ask you to speak your questions into the micro-phone that's been placed here at the front, please.'

There was a shuffling of seats and several people formed an orderly queue at a stand-mike in front of the stage. Nkani had never liked microphones, so he stood up where he was and said in his gentle, yet strong, African voice, 'Sir, I have a question.'

'To the microphone, if you wouldn't mind, please.'

Nkani ignored the pinstripe and carried on, 'My question is this: sir, you seem to know a lot about the subject of AIDS. Your knowledge is certainly very impressive. But have you *listened* to those who are suffering? I mean, have you *really* listened to them, or have you just read about them?'

There was suddenly a sense of tension in the hall. The pinstripe shuffled nervously and smiled patronizingly at the questioner who should have been at the microphone. He leaned towards the microphone, but the Speaker moved in first. It was all right. He was used to this. He could handle it.

'Yes, I'd like to thank my friend for asking this important question. Part of my research involved assembling a detailed questionnaire that was sent to 1000 sufferers in 17 different countries, probably including yours. As I said earlier, 78 per cent responded, which is remarkable. I can assure you, I have studied those responses very carefully and in that respect have certainly listened to them.'

The pinstripe smiled an artificial smile, put his hand on the mike stand and attempted to ask for the next question, but Nkani spoke again.

'With respect, sir, I would like to invite you to meet the sufferers in my country. You cannot meet people through a questionnaire. People from my country will not open their heart in a questionnaire. They have a voice that has become so weak that you have to draw close to hear them. Sometimes it is no more than a whisper. Please, will you travel with me to my home village? You would be my guest, and there you could listen. I think it would help.'

The pinstripe was now sweating. This was not the kind of 'question' he had wanted at all. In fact, he had never had anyone behave like this. The conference had gone so smoothly up to this point. He leaned toward the Speaker and said something that no one could hear. Then he turned back to Nkani and said, 'You must appreciate that our speaker is a very busy man, and I very much doubt…' He failed to finish, as the Speaker leaned forward over the lectern and said, 'I will leave an e-mail address with you. Please contact me.' He smiled a quick smile and then looked hastily toward the queue of other questioners, raising his eyebrows in anticipation of a rather more helpful question.

'Thank you, sir,' said Nkani quite fearlessly, 'but I think I should talk with you afterwards, as I have a better idea. There won't be any problems. I will meet you at the back of the hall before you leave', and the breadth of his smile spoke not of victory but of an inner joy that, as far as he was concerned, a friendship had been formed.

Thus it was that, six weeks later, the Speaker found himself, against all his better judgment, settling into his Business Class seat on a South African Airways jet. He was shuffling several sheets of paper but not reading any of them. He could not for the life of him work out why he had agreed to go on this trip. He was even paying for it out of his own pocket! 'But it will sound impressive,' he convinced himself. 'I will at least be able to say, "When I was in Africa I witnessed first hand…" Mmm, yes, that will certainly give me more authority. It's only a week anyway. I'll treat it as a bit of a holiday. Should be fine.' But, despite his reassurances to himself, he felt rather vulnerable, as vulnerable as he had felt on the day when Nkani had asked that question in front of the whole conference and he had detected tears in Nkani's eyes when he said that the voice of his people had grown weak.

The Speaker quickly swallowed the feeling and ordered a gin and tonic from the flight attendant. When the cabin lights were dimmed, he fell into a restless sleep, one interrupted by strange dreams as he flew over the hills and valleys of Africa.

Chapter 2

TO EXPERIENCE
HOSPITALITY

To talk without listening is like
Leaving guests waiting outside.
Yet deep in the human heart is the need
To experience hospitality.

When I am leading an introductory Christian Listener training course, I follow our normal routine, which is to ask people to think of a time in their lives when they needed someone to listen to them, but the person to whom they were speaking failed to give them the listening attention they needed. No one has any difficulty in recalling such an experience, usually in their recent history. We then ask them to complete the following sentence with one word: *'When I am not listened to, I feel…'*. Meanwhile, I or my co-tutor will be poised over an overhead projector, pen in hand. The words usually flood from members of the workshop, and they are nearly always very strong words such as *hurt, angry, destroyed, lonely*. After a few moments there is a stark list of powerful feelings on the screen.

I will then ask the group to think of a time when they were well listened to, and to complete the sentence, *'When I am listened to, I feel…'*. Again, most people do not find this difficult, and I find myself writing down words such as *affirmed, empowered, respected, important*. I never fail to feel moved by this exercise. It shows the extraordinary healing power of good listening, as well as the emotional damage that can be done by the failure to listen.

I have done this exercise countless times in training seminars. I nearly always hear new words, because each individual has a very personal experience of what it is like to be well listened to, and each individual knows what it feels like when they need a listening ear and they do not receive it. In the positive list, there is one word that is nearly always offered, and that is the word 'loved'. Conversely, very often in the negative list the word 'unloved' is offered. People may not consciously link listening and love, but this exercise seldom fails to point out the connection.

Why is it that humans need to be listened to? It may seem an obvious question, but I am not convinced that we have sufficiently explored it. 'It's good to talk', ran the old BT advert. Humans do need to talk. Clearly there is a range of personality types and social cultures, and the quantity of talking varies between them, but the vast majority of people choose to talk and spend much time in talking. I am not a psychologist, so I am not going to delve into the complexities of human verbal communication. Rather, I am interested in what happens to us when good-quality listening is offered as the context for our talking.

'I WANT TO TALK'

There's a phrase that seems to crop up in many films and soap operas. It is normally used by a woman who has a problem and needs her man to listen in such a way that deeper communication can take place. So she says, 'Frank, I want to talk—I mean really talk.' It is a signal that communication must go to a deeper level than normal everyday chat about what to pick up from the shops or why the government has got it wrong.

Frank now has a variety of possible responses. The first is, 'Sure, Anne, honey, I'm home early this evening, how about then?' That's the Frank who is well organized and lives life in a fairly compartmentalized way, so this is another appointment for the diary. Anne is left feeling that an important moment has passed: she is reduced to being an item in Frank's very busy schedule, and she will be another unwanted pressure in his day at a time when what he really wants is to settle down with a beer and watch the football. Another response might be, 'Oh Anne, honey, it's fine. Let's go out for a film tonight.' Frank's warning buzzer goes off: that kind of language from Anne indicates a problem. Needs fixing. Try film. May need flowers. Another response from a technological Frank might be a development of this. A blue screen comes up in his mind—'Anne has performed an illegal function'—and he looks for an equivalent Ctrl-Alt-Del action that will close down this action of Anne's, because it has broken a code of conduct that keeps things ticking over nicely, albeit at a superficial level. Other Franks might well offer an angry response, and there can be sad stories of domestic violence ensuing from simple requests for real communication.

Just occasionally, however, Frank may stop what he's doing, sit down with her and say, 'OK, tell me, what is it?' and we are treated to the rare spectacle of someone offering real quality listening.

Most of us get by in everyday life through fairly superficial conversation that serves its purpose of keeping us in touch with others and getting things done. Even at this level, good listening can make a world of difference. It is at the deeper, personal levels, however, that the costs of poor listening can be so high and the effects of good listening can be so healing.

Every person has stories within them that need telling. At certain points in life, they can feel an urgent need to tell one of these stories. Somebody who is grieving, for example, often wants to tell their story of loss. They probably won't know why they need to tell the story; it is simply there, at the back of the throat, and it must be spoken out. 'Talking it out' is nearly always a very important part of the therapy needed by somebody wounded by loss. Why does telling the story help? Why can't we just keep it inside us? What is it about the human that has been designed to speak out the stories within? We will each have our personal answers to these questions. I have been exploring mine.

I have been trying to listen to myself. What do I do when I feel a problem pressing on my soul and I need some kind of solution or resolution? I've learned that my way is to have a chat with myself first. If possible, I like to go out for a walk. I'm sure there must be times when I am talking out loud, so I just hope people don't draw the wrong conclusions! I do worry sometimes that I might be like Reggie Perrin (that wonderful challenger of the system who blessed our TV screens in the 1970s) who, in his railway compartment, would occasionally blurt out a fragment of the imaginary conversation going on in his head, thus bemusing his fellow passengers. So far, though, I like to think that I carry on my own imaginary conversations in a fairly sane way. I want to talk it out with God as well but, despite my strong belief that God speaks back to me, my hearing is still very poor, so it can all too easily be a one-way conversation. I find that this telling of my story to myself and to God does help, but it feels incomplete. Sooner or later I need another human, and that other human needs to be someone who will listen.

So what happens when I am in the company of a good listener? This is often the point where I start to make some headway. I begin to clarify my thinking and I can see some of the decisions I need to take, some of the options open to me—and this is long before my listening friends offer their insights. More and more I am coming to the conviction that the best solution to our problems may be formed within our own souls. Other people may suggest solutions, or parts of the solution, through the advice they offer, but these won't be tailor-made for me. Only I can provide a tailor-made solution. But—and this is the important part—I find it very difficult to find my own solution without the help of a listener. It is as if I have to journey to a deeper part of myself, and to embark on that journey I need company. In this way, the listening friend is not so much giving me a solution as giving me the companionship I need to venture in and discover the solution for myself.

There are other life situations in which I find myself, where I want to tell my story, not so much to find a solution but because the telling of the story 'gets it out of my system'. To have it locked up feels like a pressure within. Grieving is just such a situation. When I lost a number of friends through cancer in a short period of time, I did not need solutions. The only solution that could have helped me would have been the return of my friends. I did need listeners, though—people who were prepared to hear my story without being bored by it, and who would allow me to talk until I had talked enough. I needed people who could still accept me in all my human frailty.

Acceptance is even more important if the story I am telling is one of which I feel ashamed. We can often have experiences that we need to talk about, but which betray our fears, longings, anxieties, doubts, temptations. We should choose our listeners very carefully when we tell such stories, and it can feel risky. It can be a very bruising experience to share our weakness and then be met by a judgmental frown, a disapproving comment or a piece of advice that implies I could/should do better, because it is the vulnerable part of us that gets hit.

In my personal experience, then, the companionship of a listening friend is essential for me to express my story, whether it is a story that needs a solution or a story that I simply need to tell because it is too painful to keep locked up. And this tells me much about our humanity.

HUMANS IN COMMUNITY

As humans we have been designed for community, and this is abundantly clear as far back as the Genesis creation narratives. In the Genesis 1 account, the pronoun 'we' is consistently used of God's creative acts, and for Christians this is a clear reference to the divine community of Father, Son and Holy Spirit. When it comes to creating humans, therefore, we are told that God the Trinity says, 'Let us make humankind in our own image', and proceeds to create them 'male and female', calling them to 'be fruitful and multiply' (vv. 26–28). Inherent in the creation of humans is the fact that we have been made in and for community. In Genesis 2:18 we have the words, 'It is not good that the man should be alone.' It is written almost as if God is studying and observing what he has made and, as he watches the man walking in his freshly made world, he realizes that although he has made everything good, this aloneness is not good.

There is an almost comical side to the account of the finding of a suitable companion for Adam, as the Lord brings him various creatures that have been formed from the ground, and of course none of them is suitable as a partner. It is only when God forms the woman from Adam's own body that the partner is found, when Adam can say 'bone of my bones and flesh of my flesh' (2:18–23). Although there is clear reference here to the most intimate of human relationships, it is nonetheless a signal that humans have been created in community, and so that is the place of well-being.

Listening is fundamentally an expression of this community, as without it community would not exist. The curse in the tower of Babel story in Genesis 11 is when God says, 'Let us go down, and confuse their language there, so that they will not understand one another's speech' (v. 7). The great fear of the people of Babel was that they might be scattered. Ironically, the result of their separate languages is that this fear comes to pass. The different languages did not stop them speaking and telling their stories. God did not make them dumb. The terrible consequence was that no one could under-stand them: that is, there was no one who could listen to them. This is the curse of Babel—to have no one to listen to you. It is the place where we feel cut off, out of community, alone and scattered. It is the opposite of that God-intended experience of being able to say, 'bone of my bones and flesh of my flesh'.

This is the real pain of not being listened to: we feel 'scattered'. We feel that there is nobody who understands. We may tell our story but, to use the image of the parable of the sower, it feels as though the seed has fallen on the path and the rocky places, rather than the receptive place of the good soil (Matthew 13:1–9). People cannot understand our 'language', and we are left feeling very much alone. Right at the heart of the early Genesis stories we see the fundamental need for humans to live in community, and for the quality of listening to be central to this life. We also see the tragic effects of loss of community, and loss of listening companions.

A friend of mine, David, cares for young men who are ex-offenders. He is wonderfully committed to these young men and builds small community households for them where they can learn to rebuild their lives. He was recently part of a Christian Listening training workshop that I was leading. After the workshop, he came up to me full of enthusiasm for what he had learned. Then, with a sorrowful face, he told me how most of the young men in his care had never ever received quality listening. They had no real concept of a conversation. If he was talking with someone, another might easily barge in and not even register that something important was happening in that human interaction. David was not saying this as a complaint against these young men—simply as a sad observation.

It is a sobering thought that there are parts of our society where people have no idea of what it is like to be listened to, and because they are not listened to, they often have to resort to screaming and violence. Martin Luther King once said that rioting was the voice of the unheard. To be deprived of a listening ear causes deep suffering: 'When I am not listened to, I feel hurt, angry, destroyed, lonely.' No wonder they resort to something noisy, whether it be expressed through a ghetto-blaster, screaming in the streets or loud graffiti. Part of the hospitality that David offers these young men is a listening ear, but it is such a new experience for some that it is very disturbing.

All this is in contrast to what I encountered in South Africa. Intrinsic to the white British mentality is speaking: we have a lot to say. We are descendants of a nation that once ruled large parts of the world. The Victorian Englishman (and I do use 'English' and 'man' deliberately) saw himself as one whose task in life was to put others right. He moved into other people's countries, often with the best of intentions, and told them how to live. Listening to local customs does not often feature large in the mind of the conqueror. It is well known that much missionary activity, courageous as it was, was closely bound up with 'civilizing' people.

The legacy in South Africa is particularly tragic, although healing is now taking place. The black people of South Africa have had a number of invasions by white peoples, and during the years of apartheid they suffered the ultimate indignity of being treated as a lesser expression of the human race. While in Cape Town, I met one of our black Christian Listener tutors who lives in one of the city's townships. Although apartheid had been dismantled for several years, and a whole new era had begun, she was still aware of the pains of the past. She told me how many black folk were never listened to by white people. 'It was assumed that black people had nothing relevant or important to say,' she said sadly, but then added, 'and this is why it still feels like a healing every time a white person listens to me.'

She told me how listening has always been an important part of black community life. If you ask someone, 'How are you?' in the township, you may need to allow half a day for the answer! She also told me of one township custom that is quite common. Someone starts to tell a personal story. As others realize that this is an important story, and one that the person needs to tell, they stop what they are doing and come and listen. All listen with great respect, giving the storyteller all the time they need. After they have finished, another person may feel that the telling has connected with a story of their own, so they begin to tell theirs, and so it goes on. This is known as a *Ndaba*, and it can go on for several days.

I sometimes wonder whether this quality of 'listening hospitality' is one of the reasons why Nelson Mandela was able to lead the South African black majority so well and relatively peacefully in those huge days of upheaval and transition in the 1990s. In his book *Long Walk to Freedom*, he writes of his early life in his home village. When he was nine years old, his father died, and the result of this was that his mother took the young Nelson to the local chief who had offered to become his guardian. Thus it was that he grew up in the world of this regent and became fascinated with the way justice was carried out—a fascination that was to influence his choice of career as a lawyer. As a child, he watched with interest the tribal meetings that were carried out in the 'Great Place', where the chief and his leaders met. He writes, 'As a leader I have always followed the principles I first saw demonstrated by the regent at the Great Place. I have always endeavoured to listen to what each and every person in a discussion had to say before venturing my own opinion.'[2]

Such a comment reveals the high value placed on listening to everyone in the community. It is one of the reasons why a sense of community is so strong in black South African culture and, conversely, the inability to listen is one of the reasons why many communities here in the UK are so fragmented.

Recently, one of our Christian Listeners in South Africa referred me to an article written by Margaret Wheatley soon after 11 September 2001.[3] Margaret is a South African writer and speaker on community and communication. In this article, entitled 'Listening as Healing', she writes about a young black South African woman who taught a profound lesson in listening:

She was sitting in a circle of women from many nations, and each woman had the chance to tell a story from her life. When her turn came, she began quietly to tell a story of true horror—of how she had found her grand-parents slaughtered in their village. Many of the women were Westerners, and in the presence of such pain, they instinctively wanted to do some-thing. They wanted to fix, to make it better, anything to remove the pain of this tragedy from such a young life. The young woman felt their compassion, but also felt them closing in. She put her hands up, as if to push back their desire to help. She said: 'I don't need you to fix me. I just need you to listen to me.'

Margaret goes on to talk about the experiences of the Truth and Reconciliation Commission hearings in South Africa. Many who gave testimony at these hearings acknowledged the healing nature of telling their story to a group of people who were willing to listen.

One young man who had been blinded after being shot by a policeman said, 'I feel what has been making me sick all the time is the fact that I couldn't tell my story. But now it feels like I've got my sight back by coming here and telling you the story.'

'So why is being heard so healing?' asks Margaret Wheatley.

I don't know the full answer to that question, but I do know it has something to do with the fact that listening creates relationship... Everybody has a story, and everybody wants to tell their story in order to connect... Listening moves us closer, it helps us become more whole, more healthy, more holy. Not listening creates fragmentation, and fragmentation is the root or all suffering.

The people of Babel experienced that fragmentation, that scattering. They had no one who could listen to them. What they desperately needed was a community in which they could find those who would listen to their stories. Thus listening is a vital part of community life.

LISTENING AND LOVE

My first real experience of Christian community was just after leaving university, when I spent a year in an extended Christian household in the village of Cuddington in Buckinghamshire. This household was based around the family of John and Ros Harding, and there were other Christian households in the village that formed the community. It was an extremely formative year for me, and one that gave me the opportunity to share in caring activity for people with many kinds of needs. While at university, I had studied Dietrich Bonhoeffer as part of my degree in theology. I was particularly taken by his book *Life Together*, which he wrote while leading a small seminary of the German 'Confessing Church' at Finkenwalde. In fact, it was much more than a seminary, as Bonhoeffer sought to build an expression of authentic Christian community based on the teaching of the Sermon on the Mount. There was something very poignant about this community, a vulnerable protest movement on the eve of war. I returned to the book while I was living in community myself and found it most relevant to my own experience. I still continue to find it one of the most inspiring books on my rather overcrowded bookshelves.

In a chapter on 'Ministry', Bonhoeffer includes a section on 'the ministry of listening', where he writes:

The first service that one owes to others in the fellowship consists in listening to them. Just as the love of God begins with listening to his word, so the beginning of love for the brethren is learning to listen to them. It is God's love for us that he not only gives us his Word but also lends his ear... Christians, especially ministers, so often think they must always contribute something when they are in the company of others, that this is one service they have to render. They forget that listening can be a greater service than speaking... Christians have forgotten that the ministry of listening has been committed to them by him who is himself the great listener and whose work they should share. We should listen with ears of God that we may speak the Word of God.[4]

I still continue to marvel at these words. I think of this great theologian and hero of faith, who had so much to say and write, yet he laid great emphasis on listening, because he saw a very close link between listening and love.

It is well known that the New Testament uses different Greek words for 'love' and it is a pity that, in the English language, we have just the one word for such a range of experience. There are many different nuances in the Greek words for 'love' but, very generally speaking, if you look at two of the most commonly used in the New Testament, it is evident that *eros* is basically a love motivated by personal desire, and *agapé* is a love motivated by self-giving. Thus, 'love' as it is commonly used in a romantic film usually means *eros*. A man loves a woman because he is besotted with her and vice versa. 'I love you' can easily mean 'I want you'.

Agapé love is much harder to find. Perhaps that old film, *Love*

Story, shows something of *agapé* love. Here the boy meets the girl and falls in love, which begins as *eros* love. Then the whole tenor of the film changes when it becomes clear that the girl is dying. *Eros* love would give up at this point and go away, saying, 'I'm only going to get pain out of this. I quit now', but *agapé* love stays put. The boy's heart has been touched with this deeper love and he stays and loves her until her untimely death.

Good listening is a very practical expression of *agapé* love. We could almost say that poor listening is connected with *eros* love, because the person listens simply for what they can get out of the relationship. Good listening, however, says, 'I'm here as a listener for you, providing a safe place for you to tell your story.' In reality, good listeners are often rewarded, but that is not the primary reason why they listen. They listen so that someone else can grow, and this is a true mark of *agapé* love. This, I think, is why so few practise good listening. In today's consumer society, we have forgotten what self-giving love is all about. Yet isn't this the kind of love that God shows to us? And are we not required to love one another as he has loved us? (John 13:34).

THE GREAT LISTENER

Bonhoeffer calls God 'the great listener', and if we look at the New Testament we see that God incarnate in Jesus certainly does have exceptional listening qualities. Let's consider two stories in Luke's Gospel.

The first is the rather intriguing account of Simeon in Luke 2:25–35. Here is the story of a man who is something of a mystic and a prophet. His name suggests he is a listener, as 'Simeon' means 'one who listens'. Jacob's wife Leah called her son Simeon, because, as recorded in Genesis 29:33, she said that the Lord had heard her. The Simeon in Luke's story is true to his name, for he has been carefully listening to the Lord. Not only that, but he is a listener upon whom the Holy Spirit is resting.

It was Bishop John Taylor who coined the phrase 'the go-between God' about the Holy Spirit—a wonderfully descriptive title that tells us much about the Holy Spirit's role in communication. It was the Spirit on the day of Pentecost who enabled the disciples to proclaim the good news in languages that all could understand—a direct counter-blessing to the terrible curse of Babel. When the Spirit is around, not only is good news proclaimed, but God is heard. Five of the gifts of the Spirit listed in 1 Corinthians 12 are related to quickening our natural abilities to listen (wisdom, knowledge, prophecy, discernment and interpretation of tongues). Thus Simeon the listener has known an empowering of his natural ability to listen well. He has heard God say, 'Simeon, you won't die before you see the Christ', and now he inspects everyone who enters the temple, on the look-out and listen-out. He is waiting for a prompting of the Spirit and, sure enough, one day he feels that prompting. He sees a child, and he senses in his spirit that this is *the* child. Luke tells us, 'Guided by the Spirit, Simeon came into the temple' (2:27). This is a wonderful verse for meditation. If only we were as open to the Spirit, how often would we know him ushering us into the temple, a place of sensing the presence of God?

I have a suspicion that Simeon lived so close to the Spirit that all he needed was a whisper, a still small voice. One of my regular sorrows is the thought that the Spirit often wants to guide me, and yet I am too busy, too preoccupied, too deaf to hear his prompting. That was not Simeon's problem. He hears, he responds and he finds himself standing by a young mother who is presenting her beloved son to God.

Simeon asks to hold the baby, and Mary, who herself has proved that she is no fool when it comes to listening to God, no doubt realizes that this is a special moment. As Simeon holds the infant Jesus, he prophesies (vv. 34–35). Prophecy is no more or less than the speaking out of what you have heard, so it is rooted in listening. In many church circles, prophecy is seen as fundamentally un-reliable, but this is because, all too often, the person giving the prophecy has not learned how to listen. In my experience it often takes a wounded heart to become open to prophetic words from God. I suspect that Simeon's heart held wounds, and as he held the child he became aware of the themes of both glory and suffering. One of the things he says about Jesus is that 'the thoughts of many hearts will be revealed' (v. 35, NIV). The Greek word for 'thought' is *dialogismos*, which literally means 'thought, reasoning or inward questioning'. Simeon sensed that Jesus' ministry would reveal the 'thoughts, reasoning and inward questionings' of the heart. Note that he refers to the heart here, not the mind or soul. The heart, *kardia*, is a word used in the New Testament to mean the very centre of us—the seat of the intellect, will and emotions, the place where these qualities come together and make me the person I am. According to Simeon's prophecy, there was going to be something about Jesus that would reveal the thoughts, reasoning and inward questionings of the deepest and most central place of people's lives. As we explore more of the stories in Luke's Gospel, we see that this is exactly what happens.

One of the best-known stories comes right at the end of Luke's Gospel, and it makes very clear the ability of Jesus to reveal the deep places of the heart. In Luke 24 we have the story of the two friends who walk to Emmaus on what is the first Easter Day, although they don't know it. They are very depressed, still in the early stages of grief after the death of Jesus. Unbeknown to them, Jesus has risen and actually comes to walk beside them. In verse 17 he asks them, 'What are you discussing?' In the middle of their grief, they pour out their story to Jesus. Here Jesus models the excellent listener: he gives them space in which to tell everything. They give Jesus the facts, and they share their feelings.

Jesus then does something that is actually against Christian Listener rules: he tells them that they are foolish! When I read this, I couldn't help feeling that this is the worst possible thing to do after someone has made themselves vulnerable by sharing their sorrow. Yet it doesn't seem to put the disciples off, because later they say to one another, 'Were not our hearts burning within us while he was talking to us on the road, while he was opening the scriptures to us?' (v. 32). So was Jesus breaking a cardinal rule of Christian listening, or is something deeper happening here?

I find myself reflecting again on what Jesus said to them: 'How foolish you are, and how slow of heart to believe' (v. 25). There's that word 'heart' again. In other words, he is saying that they have read the scriptures but have not taken them into their hearts. They have listened to the scriptures, yes, but only at a superficial level. Like the seed that fell along the path in the parable of the sower, it did not reach the centre of their lives, where the good soil of faith resides. Foolishness is the opposite of wisdom and, as we shall see later, wisdom is very closely connected to listening. Jesus is using words carefully here, as ever. He is helping the disciples to realize that part of their suffering is due to the fact that they have not listened wisely to the scriptures, and as a result their hearts have found it very hard to believe. Just in passing, it is interesting to note that believing is not merely an activity of a cerebral part of us: it happens in the very depths of our beings.

As the disciples listen to Jesus, they begin to open their hearts to the scriptures and, as they do this, their hearts start catching fire. I see a process happening here: Jesus comes and listens to their story. He listens in such a way that the disciples are able to share their hearts—their thoughts, reasonings and inward questionings. They are also made aware of the fact that they have failed to listen to the voice of God through the scriptures in the past: they have not let God's word go deeply into them. They have not applied wisdom, and as a result they have suffered from misconceptions. Now, having had their bad news listened to, they become open to hearing the good news.

Jesus models for us the important principle that if we are to share the good news, we must first be prepared to listen to the bad news. As Bonhoeffer wrote, we need to learn to listen with the ears of God before we speak the word of God. Very often, people can't hear the good news until they have had a chance to tell their story. The concluding part of this process is that being well listened to affects these disciples' hearts. They have been able to express what is on their hearts; they have heard what is inside themselves. Now they can truly hear the word of God, and the word is so relevant to them, and such good news, that their hearts catch fire.

It was Henri Nouwen who said that listening is the highest form of hospitality.' It is not insignificant that the Emmaus episode ends with a story of hospitality and Jesus breaking bread (Luke 24:30). When we offer good-quality listening to someone, it is like saying, 'Come in; settle down. Here is a safe place for you to tell your story.' It doesn't have to happen in a counselling room or on the therapist's couch. At any moment in the day we can offer such hospitality, and when we do we are immediately opening a door of healing for the other person, and the God-inspired therapies of community life start to take effect. Listening is indeed a precious gift for a wounded world of scattered people.

THE SPEAKER (2)

He wasn't expecting rain as he arrived. He thought Africa would be hot and dusty. He felt a bit put out. And there was a delay with the baggage. He complained to a smartly dressed lady, who informed him that he would not have to wait long. But he did have to wait long. He watched the unmoving luggage carousel, waiting, waiting. Then after a piercing siren it shuddered into life, and the heaving group of hopefuls moved towards it with their empty trolleys, looking keenly for familiar signs of home. Wearily, they each pulled their bags from the carousel—each, that is, except the Speaker. He was left alone, watching two cases going on their pointless journey, cases that were not his. His had not arrived. He sighed with irritation and snapped at the attendant as he filled out the necessary forms. The attendant looked at the address of where he was staying. 'It might take a day or two to get your luggage there, sir,' she said rather defensively. She knew all too well what would come next, and it did—an important man making the case that he was a special case, and his case was a special case that should be delivered with urgency. After many 'yes, sirs', she filed the papers away and watched the ruffled Englishman walk through Customs with nothing to declare, for he had no suitcase.

Nkani was delighted to see him. He had half wondered if the Speaker would find some excuse, and not come. But he was here, and Nkani was thrilled and smiled the broadest smile. The Speaker was not smiling. He told Nkani about his suitcase, and Nkani roared with laughter. It was very funny. Funny things often happened in Africa. The Speaker did not find it funny. He had to hold on to his anger, or else his sense of vulnerability would rise to the surface. It was one thing to leave the comforts of home and venture into the Third World; it was quite another to go without your support system. So he said very little as Nkani's borrowed car drove away from the smart airport along many miles of road, each road becoming less smart, less tarmacked, more rough, so that by the end the car was travelling very slowly as Nkani steered it around cavernous potholes.

'Where the hell are you taking me?' asked the grumpy Speaker.

'To my home—it is not far now,' replied the serene Nkani, who loved driving. For him it was a special treat, and he was grateful to his good friend Mosha for lending him his old car. Mosha was too weak to drive now, and he was going to let Nkani have it when he died. Nkani hoped he would live for many years yet, but he knew that Mosha was not looking well. The cross that Nkani had given his friend when they were teenagers hung from the rear-view mirror, and clunked against the windscreen as the car jolted on its muddy journey. He glanced across at the Speaker, who was tightly clutching the handle above the passenger window to steady himself. Nkani saw his white cuffs protruding from his suit jacket. There was something made of gold attached to the cuff. This was the first time Nkani realized that the man must be wealthy. Curiously, it was at that moment that the Speaker said, 'Nkani, I'll need to get to a bank soon—tomorrow will do.'

'Of course,' said Nkani, a response he and his friends always made when faced with a problem.

'This is your room,' said Martha, Nkani's wife. The Speaker had barely noticed her when Nkani introduced her. He was relieved to get out of the noisy, rattling cage of the vehicle that he had had to travel in, and he was relieved to discover that he had a private room.

'Can you tell me where your bathroom is?' he snapped.

'Our toilet is just down this track,' said Nkani, remarkably casually.

'Down the track?' asked the astonished Speaker. 'Which track?'

'The track from the back door,' said Nkani. 'Our toilets are outside here. But there is a bowl in your room if you prefer.'

The Speaker now felt quite panicky, but he did not want to show it. 'Oh, fine. Um, what about a shower?'

'Yes, I'll get it arranged,' said Nkani kindly. He was aware that this was difficult for the Englishman. He wished he could offer him a more comfortable house. 'I'm sorry,' he said in a way that made the Speaker stop his frantic quest for comfort. For the first time since he had arrived, he looked at Nkani. He was a tall man, young—early 20s, very dark-skinned, handsome with a dignified face. For a moment, the Speaker saw sadness in those dark eyes, and he felt a stab of discomfort that he might have insulted his host.

'You have a very pleasant house, Nkani,' said the Speaker. Nkani breathed in and looked at Martha and smiled. It meant a lot to him that the Englishman should like his home.

Nkani rigged the shower up—a bucket with holes in it, which was hoisted up outside in a small brick enclosure that served as a bathroom. He warmed some water on the stove and, when he felt the temperature was just right, he gave the Speaker a generous supply. He also found a shirt, some trousers and underwear to lend to the Speaker until his suitcase should arrive.

While the Speaker was showering, Martha led Nkani out of the house, and sat with him on a piece of unfinished wall. 'Nkani,' she said, stroking his hand with her long, delicate fingers. Nkani watched her fingers, wondering what news required them to converse out-side. A drop of water landed on his hand. He looked to the sky, but there was no cloud in the dark blue expanse. The heavy showers were over and it was hot now.

'Nkani,' said Martha again, and as he looked at his beloved wife, he saw that the drop of water was coming not from the sky but from her cloudy eyes. 'We got the news this morning, when you were at the airport.'

'Oh no,' said Nkani. 'Oh no, not so soon.'

'I'm sorry,' said Martha, 'He... it was during the night.'

'My dear friend...' said Nkani, and buried his burning face into Martha's shoulder. As she held him, she swayed and hummed a song they both knew well. It was a song of hope—but how brittle hope seemed sometimes.

Chapter 3

TO UNLOCK THE DOOR

To listen to another
Causes us to pause:
In those moments there is an opportunity
To unlock the door.

As I was preparing to write this chapter, I came across a fascinating article in *The Times* by Rabbi Jonathan Sacks, who is well known for his thoughtful writings and stimulating talks. His article is entitled 'Listening is the greatest gift we can give to a troubled soul'.[5] That in itself is a remarkable statement. He opens his article with a story about the psychotherapist Viktor Frankl, a survivor of Dachau and Auschwitz, who developed a new school of psychotherapy called Logotherapy, based on finding meaning in suffering. One night, Frankl was woken by a phone call from a client who told him that she was about to commit suicide. They had a long conversation during which Frankl offered her many reasons to carry on living. At the end of the call, the woman said she felt much better and assured Frankl that she would not take her life. She was true to her word and, when they met some time later, Frankl asked which of his reasons had persuaded her. He was somewhat surprised, and no doubt a little put out, when she said that it was not his reasons that had made any difference to her. Sacks writes, 'Her answer was simple. Frankl had been willing to listen to her in the middle of the night. A world in which someone was prepared to listen to another's distress seemed to her one in which it was worthwhile to live.' He goes on to say:

What an underrated art listening is. Sometimes it is the greatest gift we can give to a troubled soul. It is an act of focused attention. It means being genuinely open to another person, prepared to enter their world, their perspective, their pain. It does not mean we have a solution to their problem. There are some problems that cannot be solved. They can only be lived through, so that time itself heals the rupture or loss. When we listen we share the burden so its weight can be borne. There are times when friendship calls simply for a human presence, a listening ear and an understanding heart, so that soul can unburden to soul.

He ends his excellent article with the simple yet profound statement, 'Listening is where pain is healed by being shared'. Rabbi Sacks has grasped the extraordinarily therapeutic nature of listening. If he has such insights about listening, he may well have known the experience of being listened to well, and he may have taken the risk of listening well to others. To some extent, it is assuredly a risk.

I have already mentioned that I am indebted to Dr Frank Lake for his inspiring lectures at St John's College, and also for all that I learned from the organization he set up, initially called Clinical Theology and now known as The Bridge Pastoral Foundation.[6] One of Frank's papers that I have found particularly helpful is *Listening and Responding*, a typical mix of insightful theology and psychology together with practical help. Right at the beginning of this paper, Frank acknowledges that listening can be very uncomfortable: 'Listening to others humbling themselves to tell what for years they have hidden, is a burden to the listener.'

Frank argues that our culture trains us in concealment from our earliest years. We learn that sharing certain things from the depths of our being can be met with anger, rejection, misunderstanding and other expressions of hostility. It is important, of course, that we learn to distinguish between what is safe to share and what is unsafe. Sadly, this means that too many stories remain trapped inside us, a situation that can lead to many symptoms of dis-ease. If, then, you are a person who is listening to some of that trapped material, especially if you are one of the first to hear it, you can easily feel overwhelmed. You may well be anxious about where it is going to lead. Will the person lose control and start crying all over you? Will they be emotionally disabled by the telling and expect you to put them together again? Will they start disclosing material that will be a burden for you to carry? All kinds of anxieties can come into play when we start listening to others.

At Acorn, we recently started to share our listening training with the Chinese community in Hong Kong, and we encountered an interesting cultural problem, to do with a social agreement about avoiding public vulnerability. Not only is the person speaking ashamed if they share what they consider to be a deep weakness, but it also puts the listener into a very difficult situation. The listener becomes anxious that their listening has encouraged the speaker to share something shameful. The Acorn staff working in Hong Kong want to respect this cultural tradition, while at the same time introducing people to the trans-cultural healing effect of good listening. It is not easy!

IVORY TOWERS

As we learn to listen, we have to face those parts of ourselves that become uncomfortable as people start to tell their story to us. In Acorn's *Just Listen!* training video, a number of 'ivory towers' have been identified—places that we may retreat to, thereby preventing us from listening to others. If we are to listen well to others, we will need to recognize these towers, dare to come down, unlock the door and find healing for ourselves by listening to others. Some of the most common ones are the 'I can't fix it' tower, the 'I may upset them' tower and the 'Listening is a woman's job' tower.

'I can't fix it'

Some of us are poor listeners because we assume that if we start listening to someone sharing their problems, we will have to provide a solution. We imagine ourselves in a scenario where some poor soul has unburdened themselves and, after describing their sad tale, they look up pleadingly at us and ask, 'So what should I do?' We suddenly have to think of a brilliant solution to their problem, carrying within us a lurking fear that if we fail to do so, they will be immensely disappointed. We may feel as if the sufferer has emotionally unravelled themselves in front of us, so that we are unable to gather them up again.

If you find yourself thinking in this way, then dare to explore it a bit further. Maybe you will find a kind of 'Messiah complex' within you. Many of us who are clergy are all too familiar with this idea. 'Of course we're not the Messiah,' we quickly retort, outraged at the theological implications of such cheekiness. And yet, in terms of our behaviour, we actually behave as messiahs. We feel we must have a solution to every problem in the church, an appropriate word of comfort for every distressed individual, an evangelistic message that is an exact fit for every unbeliever we meet, and a perfectly crafted prayer for every sick person who limps forward at a healing service. After all, we have been trained! We were given a 'tool-kit' at college, and we are there to sort the problems. Such thinking has been at the root of too many clergy breakdowns.

Some years back, I led a residential listening course for clergy. After an intensive three days, we came to the last session where each person was invited to share with the group something that they had learned on the course. One vicar spoke most honestly and movingly. He told us how, when he first started out in the ordained ministry, he did listen to people. Some time ago, however, he took the decision to listen no longer. He could not bear to hear people's problems when he couldn't think of any solutions. He somehow felt fraudulent as a minister and certain that he was letting down the person concerned.

During the listening course, though, he had a 'conversion moment'. He suddenly discovered that it was OK to listen without having a solution to the problem being described. He realized that the person speaking to him seldom spoke with the assumption that he would be able to 'sort them out', and even if they did assume that, he could find a way to explain that he was providing listening space, not an advice service. He also saw for himself, during the listening course, that people who did start sharing their problems with a good listener seldom wanted that listener to give a solution. What they needed was a chance to tell their story and so be empowered to find their own way forward. For this vicar, that realization was a deep healing. He was able to become more human again. He was able to enter into community at a deeper level again. For him, learning to listen brought the reward of inner healing.

'I may upset them'

Some of us have come from homes where there was a free expression of emotions, and others are from homes where emotions had to be well controlled. Some of us have come from homes where emotions were freely expressed in a safe way. Others had experiences in childhood where we saw the consequences of un-controlled emotions, such as anger. This means that we each carry into our adult life an instinctive response to the use of feelings. People who take the risk of listening to others may often find that the person speaking says, 'I never intended to tell you all this…', and such telling may lead them into an expression of their feelings, very often with tears. For those who are not used to tears, this can be quite daunting. We feel that our listening to the person has upset them. What do we do? Usually we reach for some tissues and start mopping up. We assume that the person must feel ashamed at this eruption of emotion, with the rush of tears, the runny nose and the blotchy face. We feel we must stop them, think of some reassuring words, offer to say a prayer. A well-crafted 'all-things-work-together-for-good' kind of prayer can do wonders, quickly restoring a soggy weeper back into settled smiling Christian mode.

I know all this because I've done it myself. I come from a home where we did not witness the free expression of emotions, and I have had my own journey of healing towards becoming comfortable with other people's emotions. If you were one of those whom I hurried out of their discomfort in this way, then please forgive me. I am learning—slowly but, I think, surely. I am learning that the person who has the freedom to share feelings more freely than me is a gift to me. They help me to see that it is possible to share feelings with another person and survive. You won't collapse, it is not shameful, and there is no one bearing down on you, telling you to pull yourself together.

People who have wept with me are a great gift to me. Little by little I have learned that it is not disastrous if the person I listen to starts to weep. I know now that it is very likely that these will be therapeutic tears. I am learning that rushing tissues to the person might be of practical help, but does not help emotionally if I accompany the tissues with a signal that the weeping should stop. I am learning that, in most cases, if someone has weeping to do, the kindest thing is to provide a safe place for this to take place. There can be something intrinsically healing about weeping in the presence of a non-judgmental fellow human.

I have discovered something else since I let go of my anxiety about people getting upset. When I listen to someone sharing from the depths of their heart, I have found that they are teaching me something important. They are teaching me how to navigate in the depths. I can too easily live my life in the shallows. I am fascinated by the depths, but I don't think I'm that comfortable in them. When I'm swimming in the sea, I don't like going too deep. Yes, you've got it—I like being in control.

Exploring the depths takes us out of our places of safety and control. It has been the people who have shared deeply with me, however, who have brought life to me. They remind me of Brendan, the Celtic saint who watched the sea for years, and then decided the time had come to launch out in his coracle and surrender to wind and wave to discover what lay beyond the ocean. In so doing, he was probably the first European to visit America. When I am listening to someone speaking from the depths, I am full of respect. I see them as an adventurer. Frank Lake used to say that the last great continent to be discovered was the dark continent of the subconscious. The person who starts to talk about their story of struggle or pain is an explorer, and is daring to visit the world that is just a bit beyond our conscious world. They want to know what is going on inside them. In listening to them, I am inspired and say to myself, 'I also need to explore in this way.'

Of course there are times when we are listening to someone and they start exploring at a level that is completely unfamiliar to us. We may feel really quite anxious. We may feel that, by listening to them, we are responsible for them diving to these unfamiliar places. The truth is that by daring to come down from our ivory tower and unlock the door, we are providing a meeting point with another person, so that they can feel able to explore in this way. They are doing this by their own volition, not because we have been manipulative in any way. One of the great advantages of listening is that because it is non-directive, it makes no attempt to steer or influence people. It simply provides space.

'Listening is a woman's job'

When I started to lead listening training workshops, it did not altogether surprise me to discover that many more women came along than men. Seldom at our training workshops do we get more than 25 per cent men. Often the men who do come are clergy, or are engaged in some kind of pastoral or caring work. Where are all the other men?

Imagine the scenario: a poster goes up in your church inviting you to a *Learn to Listen* course. Many women immediately see the sense of this, and sign up. A number of men wander past, have a look, but don't sign up. What goes through their minds? Probably a mixture of responses such as, 'I listen OK' (dangerous one, that), 'Don't think this is going to help me practically', and other similar responses. The one that probably crops up most frequently in the male psyche is 'Listening is a woman's kind of thing'. Yes, I know, there are men reading this who are now complaining about my stereotyping, but don't forget, you are further on in the journey than many of our fellow men, because you actually got as far as reading this book on listening!

I came across a book recently with the wonderfully provocative title of *Why Men Don't Listen and Women Can't Read Maps*. It is written by a couple, Allan and Barbara Pease, and the chapter on 'Talking and Listening' makes for very interesting reading, with sub-headings that include 'Why males can't talk proper', 'Why women are great talkers', 'Men talk silently to themselves', 'Women think aloud', 'Women talk, men feel nagged', 'Strategies for talking with men' and 'How to get a man to listen'. Their humorous yet perceptive style makes for an interesting read. They base their theories on careful research and also an assumption that we developed means of communication in our 'caveman' days that still influence us today. I like the writers' advice to a woman on how to get a man to listen:

Make a time, give him an agenda, announce a time limit and tell him you don't want solutions or plans of action. Say, 'I'd like to talk with you about my day, Allan. Would after dinner be OK? I don't need any solutions to problems—I'd just like you to listen.' Most men will agree to a request like this because it has a time, a place and an objective—all the things that appeal to the male brain. And he is not expected to do any work.[7]

It sounds rather clinical, but I sense it probably works! There is no doubt that there is something intrinsically different between male and female brains, which means that, generally speaking, we listen in different ways. Men get into trouble because they slide into fix-it mode too easily. When I was thinking through all this and the implications for our listening training (as someone put it, my attempt to 'bloke-up' Christian Listeners), I went to see my good friend Roy

McCloughry, who has researched deeply into the subject of men and written so well on it.[8] It was he who pointed out to me why listening training does not often appeal to men. Listening can be seen by men as a passive activity. For many men, being trained to listen in a non-directive, reflective way can feel like being chained to a chair and forced to listen silently to an ever-talking creature in the chair opposite. They can feel quite powerless.

That is how it can appear, but the reality, of course, is quite the reverse. Listening is far from passive. Attentive listening is creating space—it is constructive. It is not sitting passively in front of a verbal waterjet. It is actively applying often intense concentration to facilitate the person we are listening to, to help them move on in their journey.

A typical conversation between men would be discussing a football match. They go over details of players' moves, and many opinions are expressed. They would find it much harder to talk about what they would consider to be more private issues, such as how they were struggling at work. Women tend to be far more relational, and therefore more interested in how others are feeling and facing issues in their lives. As Roy put it, women have *rapport talk* and men have *report talk*. Generally speaking, men prefer to discuss the facts, whereas women have more of an interest in how the facts are affecting relationships.

Most men find it harder to monitor their interior world, and it can feel very threatening for a man to listen to someone exploring deep experiences. I mentioned above that I feel much less in control when I am 'out of my depth', and this anxiety about not being in control is a common experience for men. For many men today, it feels as if the world affirms women's values, while what were traditionally considered men's values are being constantly questioned. Thank God we are in a more just society now, where women have opportunities for work that they have never had before. For men, however, this is a profound culture change. For example, when some find themselves with a female boss, they discover an inherited instinct that tells them that 'men should be in charge'. They can feel, 'If my role is no longer to be in charge, then what is it? What value do I have?' If men's traditional role has been one of control and authority, when they are encouraged to do listening training, it can feel as if they are yet again being pushed into a role that is far from the authoritative one that feels more familiar.

There are clearly huge areas for discussion here and there's not sufficient space to explore them in detail, but I do want to register that this is actually a difficult area for many men, and we can easily run up inside our male ivory tower when we are required to listen. What I have noticed over the years, though, are the rich rewards for men when we do choose to come down the tower and unlock the door. Time and again I have seen a transformation take place in men who come on listening courses. To confuse a biblical image, it is as if 'scales fall from their ears' (see Acts 9:18). Men discover that listening is not about male/female roles; it is about being human. They discover that when they risk listening to others, they often receive overwhelming gratitude. They discover routes that take them to deeper, unexplored places of their lives. They discover that, far from becoming weaker, they grow stronger. And if they are still unsure whether listening actually achieves anything, then they are more than rewarded as they see the remarkable effects of good listening.

THE EARS OF CHRIST

There is one final and very good reason for learning to listen well, and that is very simply because our Lord Jesus did it. If we are followers of Christ, then whoever we are—male or female, pastoral or evangelistic, introvert or extravert—we need to have the ears of Christ. This is not just about looking at the Gospel stories of Jesus and learning from the ways he listened deeply and therapeutic-ally to so many individuals. It is the experience of the cross that convinces us that Jesus listened in the most profound way possible. Returning to Frank Lake, who was one of the first in modern times to draw our attention to this:

God has not only spoken through his Son; what is perhaps more important, He has listened through his Son. Christ's saving work cost him most in its speechless passivity of dereliction. It is this which gives him the right to be called the greatest listener to all suffering. It is this which gives his listening its redemptive quality.[9]

We are familiar with the concept of the Word becoming flesh (John 1:14). Jesus came to this world as the Word of God. He preached the word and he was the Word, but he was a word that was spoken in the midst of the most profound listening. Among the many glorious truths of the cross is the fact that, during his sacrificial death, our Lord Jesus experienced the deepest human suffering and, in the experiencing of it, he listened. God Almighty, incarnate in his Son, listened. The Holy Spirit, the go-between God, listened. At the cross, the Holy Trinity was involved in the most profound act of listening to hurting humanity. Therefore, when we listen in Christ, we are engaged in the ministry of the cross. We too feel the vulnerability of the cross as we listen to another's story of suffering. And if the cross enables us to listen to another's suffering without running for safety up our ivory towers, it is the story of Jesus' resurrection that gives us hope for healing and renewal.

This is not an artificial healing of the easy-answer and quick-solution type. It is much more to do with an experience known by so many listeners: it is reaching that point in the listening process when the other person starts to look as if they are emerging from a dark and confusing forest—the point when they realize that there might be a way through, when they start to feel energy rise again, when they feel empowered to move on. It is a wonderful moment of hope, and the listener always feels a sense of privilege at being allowed to journey so deeply with another fellow human.

GETTING PRACTICAL

Let's suppose that you want to listen better to others. Well, there's no short cut to good training and, when you get the chance, I strongly recommend that you go on a listening course. Meanwhile, here are three suggestions that you might like to work on, to help you improve your listening skills.

1. Identify your ivory towers

Think about times when someone has wanted to talk to you, but you have felt tense and uneasy about listening to them. Can you identify what it was that prevented you? You may have had a valid reason: for example, you may have been just about to collect a child from school and you knew it would be unfair to allow your friend to start their story when you were about to leave the house. There may be other reasons why you don't always want to listen, though. I have mentioned three common 'ivory towers' in this chapter. In Acorn's *Just Listen!* course, others are discussed. Pause to reflect and see if you have one. Then imagine what it might be like to come down the tower and unlock the door. Listen carefully to your feelings, as they may give you a clue.

2. Be alert for important listening moments

Many of our conversations are a kind of to-ing and fro-ing of comments. One person says one thing, then the other another, and so on. Together they may be exchanging information, views, opinions. The point can come where one person says something significant and the other person has a choice—either to proceed in conversational mode or to let go of their own needs and focus on the other person, allowing them to tell their story. This often happens naturally but, sadly, too often the person who wants to share something important cannot do so. Have a think about these two dialogues that take place in the pub.

Geoff:	Hi, Jim, how's your day been?
Jim:	Pretty hard today, if you want the truth.
Geoff:	Oh yeah? I've had several like that this week.
Jim:	Yeah. But today was different. Stan, my boss, really laid into me.
Geoff:	Strange to say, same thing happened to me last week. I went home and told Barbara about it and she said she thought my boss was trying to lay me off.
Jim:	Well, that's just it, Geoff. I think he was trying to say that.
Geoff:	No, I'm sure he wasn't. I got worried about that, but it turned out I'd got completely the wrong message. Anyway, let's get more cheerful, shall we? Another pint?

I wonder what your reaction was as you read this. What did you feel about Geoff? What about Jim? It's the kind of conversation we have all the time. I have known times when I have wanted to speak to a friend about something important but haven't known how to signal that it really is important. I get started, but before I know where I am, we are discussing the friend's problem! Too often a friend has tried to speak to me about something important to them, and we end up talking about me or some safe objective thing 'out there' like a cricket result. Let's re-run the conversation.

Geoff:	Hi, Jim, how's your day been?
Jim:	Pretty hard today, if you want the truth.
Geoff:	Yeah? What happened?
Jim:	Oh, Stan, my boss, really laid into me.
Geoff:	What about?
Jim:	Well, because of Liz's illness, I've been getting some of my figures wrong at work, and I really mucked up a budget

I was putting together, and Stan—well, he just yelled at me and mentioned that fatal expression 'releasing you'.

Geoff: That's serious, Jim. Tell me more...

So the conversation goes on. Geoff's not offering disciplined listening, but he is applying a listening attitude. He's prepared for the focus to be on Jim. He is giving him space, and no doubt Jim will benefit from having the chance to explore how he is feeling about the crisis he is facing.

3. Try keeping your mouth shut!

Many people fail to listen because, very simply, they talk when they should be keeping quiet. To quote Dietrich Bonhoeffer again, 'Many people are looking for an ear that will listen. They do not find it among Christians, because these Christians are talking when they should be listening.'[10]

Sadly, Christians do not have a reputation for being good listeners, but we can change! Next time you listen to someone, just try resisting the temptation to jump in with untimely talk. 'Normal' conversation relies on a fairly free flow of words between people. To give focused listening means just shifting the dynamic slightly. In the first version of the story of Jim and Geoff above, Geoff cut Jim off several times by telling his own story. This often happens in conversations. Someone starts to share, and the listener responds by sharing their experience, and often we can have a very fruitful conversation based around the sharing of similar experiences. There are occasions, however, when it can be destructive, and the person wanting to share will feel very frustrated. Another tendency that many Christians have is to interject with premature reassurance. This is part of the 'fix-it' ivory tower. In the case of Jim and Geoff, it may make the conversation run like this:

Geoff: Hi, Jim, how's your day been?

Jim: Pretty hard today, if you want the truth.

Geoff: Yeah? What happened?

Jim: Oh, Stan, my boss, really laid into me.

Geoff: What about?

Jim: Well, because of Liz's illness, I've been getting some of my figures wrong at work, and I really mucked up a budget I was putting together, and Stan—well, he just yelled at me and mentioned that fatal expression 'releasing you'.

Geoff: Well, Jim, I am sure it won't get that bad. And remember, 'underneath are the everlasting arms'—God is going to take good care of you. Another pint?

There's nothing wrong with what Geoff says—it's the timing that's the problem. As caring people, we don't like seeing good friends in distress. As caring Christian people, we will want to offer spiritual resources to help the person. It is fairly clear from the example above, though, that reassurance offered before the person has really had a chance to talk makes them feel that they are being shut down. Frankly, we often do offer reassurance quickly, as we want to shut down the person in the kindest way possible. Again, it is worth taking the risk of giving more time before we apply the tissues and the reassuring comments. We may feel uneasy that we are allowing the person to suffer without offering any comfort, but the person will usually be very grateful to be given the space to explore, without that space being invaded by inaccurate words of comfort. The longer we listen, the more likely it is that, when the time does come for us to offer reassurance, it will feel far more genuine and will have the supportive effect that is intended.

Jonathan Sacks wrote that listening is where pain is healed by being shared. In my years with Acorn, I have become utterly convinced that listening truly is one of the most healing gifts that we possess. The amazing thing is that, despite the fact that it is really not difficult to learn to listen well, most of us find all kinds of 'ivory towers' to retreat to, and fail to give the level of listening that is so badly needed. As we survey our society today and see so many examples of personal pain, I can't help thinking that what we need most urgently is the gift of good listening. One of the wonderful parts of this is that both listener and speaker find healing, for when we take the opportunity to listen to another, we may well find that a door is unlocked in our heart that opens us to greater degrees of wholeness.

THE SPEAKER (3)

'I really need to get to the bank,' said the Speaker. He had not had a good night. His home seemed so far away. He missed his comfortable bed. He had spent ages getting to sleep and missed his routine of watching the evening news with a nightcap of a small Jamiesons and a bourbon biscuit. He even missed Caroline. He had not spoken to her for months. Strange that he should miss her now. But most of all, he missed his suitcase.

'I need a bank, and I need to phone the airport to find out what they have done with my damned suitcase. It's probably in Brisbane by now.' He was standing in the doorway of the kitchen, looking frankly rather ridiculous in Nkani's rather crumpled trousers and shirt, both of which were too big for him.

'Of course,' said Martha, 'but first won't you have some Weetabix?'

The Speaker struggled with this African variety of Weetabix, especially as it was doused with warm milk. He always had nice chilled milk on his Weetabix. African Weetabix was definitely not as good.

'So where is the bank?' said the Speaker.

'Nkani will talk to you about that,' said Martha.

'Well, where is he?' said the Speaker, feeling rather irritated that the man who had invited him to Africa was late for breakfast, so that he was left with this African lady whom he hardly knew. He really didn't want to make polite conversation at breakfast. It was hard enough getting the tepid cereal down, let alone exchanging niceties with somebody who probably didn't speak much English.

'Nkani is not here,' said Martha in clear English, and poured the Speaker a large mug of tea. He noticed that she put in a spoonful of sugar before he had time to tell her he didn't take any. He dreaded drinking the sweet tea and instantly worked on plans for disposing it.

'Yes, I guessed he is not here,' said the Speaker, his irritability now showing. There was a long pause and, for the first time, he took the trouble to look across the table at Martha. She smiled a very sweet smile at him, and did her best to stem the flow of tears from her large brown eyes. The Speaker felt quite panicky.

'Oh, I'm sorry. I can be a bit sharp—I do… Oh, is Nkani all right?' He felt very flustered and disorientated and, in his fluster, he sipped his horribly sweet tea and winced.

Martha picked up the large teapot and moved towards a small stove that was supporting the kettle. Suddenly she put the teapot down on the nearby windowsill. She propped her two arms on the sill and her head bent down below her shoulders. The Speaker watched her desperately trying to control herself. He felt in his trouser pocket for his handkerchief, but of course they were not his trousers and there was nothing there. He saw a little doily that was covering the sugar bowl, and handed it to Martha. She looked rather surprised, but she took it, folded it carefully in her hands and then placed it back on the breakfast table.

'I am so sorry,' she said, 'but we have many sadnesses here, and my eyes give tears for every one.'

The Speaker felt more uncomfortable than ever. If there was one thing he could not stand, it was blubbing women. He had often told Caroline about this. He could not understand why grown-up adults could not manage to control themselves properly. He knew he must stop this lady crying, but wasn't sure how. He had developed good methods with Caroline that seldom failed, but he had never had to stop a black lady crying before. He wished Nkani would come back.

In the end, he opted for changing the subject, hoping to deflect the woman from the cause of her grief, whatever it was.

'Is Nkani at work?' he asked. His question sounded very abrupt, but he did need to know where Nkani was. Nkani had the car. Nkani could get him to a bank and a telephone. He really needed Nkani.

'No, Nkani is not at work,' said Martha, who had refilled the teapot and was now back at the table. 'Nkani is grieving,' she said, and the Speaker was left to guess quite what that meant with regard to Nkani's whereabouts. Frustrated though he was, he was also struck by how dignified Martha looked. She was also probably in her early

20s. She had a round face and her black hair was tied back in a bun. The Speaker kept noticing her brilliant white teeth, especially when she smiled. She was smiling at him now.

'It is a great honour to have you in our home,' she said. 'Nkani was so pleased you accepted his invitation. We never thought we would have an English visitor here. It is very special for us.'

'Oh, it is my pleasure,' said the Speaker, not totally convincingly.

'Tell me,' said Martha, 'have you had many sadnesses this year?'

'Oh, er, one or two,' said the Speaker, not willing in the least to share such personal information with a stranger. He suddenly thought of Caroline, but quickly put her out of his mind.

'One or two?' asked Martha innocently.

'Yes,' said the Speaker, failing to understand the question.

'No, I mean have you had one sadness or two?'

The Speaker now felt anxious and was groping around for something to say, when Martha continued.

'I think you have had more than two,' she said, 'but I don't think you have had as many as we have.'

'I'm very sorry,' said the Speaker, genuinely sorry that she had had her sadnesses. 'I hope you have felt comforted.'

Martha smiled, 'I never knew that comfort had so many languages until recently.'

The Speaker was still very uncomfortable, but a bit of him was starting to surrender to the situation. However, he did have one simple task. He wanted to steer this conversation so it would end up with him knowing exactly where Nkani was. That bit of information should lead him to know how to retrieve his luggage and how to find a bank.

But suddenly he lacked energy. He sipped his sweet tea, even managing to swallow it, and, instead of pursuing his task, asked, 'What is it that you and Nkani are both sad about?'

'Do you have a best friend, sir?' asked Martha very tenderly. It was a terrible question to ask the Speaker. Why did everyone in the world have to have best friends? What was this silly obsession with friendship? He felt angry, but did not want to show it, so he lied as a shortcut.

'Yes,' he lied, curtly, and Martha knew he was not telling the truth, but she did not mind.

'Then one day you or your best friend will carry a deep burden of grief. Nkani loved Mosha as a brother. Mosha was a year younger than Nkani—only 23. He was foolish once—that's all it took. One foolish action in a moment of loneliness when he was visiting the city. One wrong thing—and now he's...' Martha did not finish her sentence. She did not want to weep. Her tears of the night were sufficient for now.

For a moment, a peace descended on the room. Martha and the Speaker sipped their tea, and all they heard was the buzzing of a fly and chickens scratching in the yard, as the hot African sun slowly climbed the blue African sky.

'Another cup of tea, sir?'

'Yes, please. Yes, that would be nice.'

Chapter 4

TO ENCOUNTER
THE UNKNOWN

When we meet one who is different
We are given a choice:
To retreat to safety
Or to encounter the unknown.

Sometimes it is distinctly uncomfortable to listen to another person. In Northern Ireland there are various groups who are making a valiant contribution to the work of reconciliation in a community that is deeply and bitterly divided. On the occasions that I have visited Belfast, I have felt profound sadness to witness the signs of prejudice and sectarianism. On my first visit, when I was taken to a Loyalist area, I was taken aback by the number of flags, and was astonished to see pavements painted with red, white and blue. I found it hard to believe that people felt the need to have such strong outward displays of the community and beliefs with which they identified.

I want to say this without judgment, because Northern Ireland has suffered from too many people looking on accusingly and saying, 'How terrible' with a sort of 'Surely they should have sorted out their differences by now' tone of voice. Northern Ireland does not have difficulties because it is full of awkward people. It has difficulties because a fundamental human weakness, one that is latent in all of us, has been engaged. The fact is that most of us, if we had grown up in Northern Ireland, would have imbibed strong feelings about 'the other side' from earliest childhood. We would have heard stories of injustice against our community from the moment we first understood language. By the time we went to junior school, we would have known well the arguments for why we were right and 'they' were wrong. The chances are that we would not have related closely to anyone from the 'other side', unless we were sent to an integrated Protestant/Catholic school. I am fairly convinced that if I had grown up in Northern Ireland, and assuming I had not experienced the healing grace of God, I would now be carrying strong feelings in my soul in support of my side and strong feelings of indignation, even hatred, against the other.

What is impressive about those committed to reconciliation in Northern Ireland is that many have a testimony of changing from prejudice to hospitality. They have made a choice not to perpetuate inherited attitudes. They have chosen to live differently. The cost for them has sometimes been high: some have even paid with their lives. It is such people who inspire me and have been teaching me that it is possible to listen to those who are different from us, even those who are our ideological enemies, and thereby to enter into a miraculous outworking of that extraordinary command of Jesus to love our enemies (Matthew 5:44).

Jean Vanier is the leader of the L'Arche community and has given much of his life to living among those with mental and intellectual disabilities, not only to care for them, but to listen to and learn from them. I first came across him in the early years of my ordained ministry, when I was struck by a magazine article he wrote entitled 'A hope that we can grow'. The magazine went out of print many years ago, but I have kept the article and still refer to it, as it is one of the best pieces of writing on community that I have ever read.[11] The thesis of this article is that 'community is not a style of life, it is the gradual realization that I am committed to people to help them to grow. Even more, it is letting them help me to grow, which is much more difficult.'

Vanier goes on to argue that those who will help me to grow most in the community are the people I find hardest to get on with. He writes, 'If I am just with those who please me, those who are doing well, I create a division in the group. It is only by being specifically attentive to those who annoy me that I become an instrument of unity.'

He then connects this conviction with a fascinating understanding of Jesus' command to love our enemies:

A disciple of Jesus Christ is one who loves the enemy. The enemy is not the national enemy or the class enemy; the enemy is the one who threatens me, the one I block off from, the one who just has to open his mouth for me to know that what he says is wrong.

We have already seen that listening is a true expression of *agapé* love. Therefore, as a disciple of Jesus I am required to listen to 'my enemy', the one who is different from me, whose values I don't share, who annoys me. It is one thing to listen to someone I like, but much harder to listen to someone I don't like, and it is even harder if that person is saying things with which I disagree. Producers of current affairs programmes often like to bring together two people with opposing views, and viewers or listeners witness a kind of verbal ping-pong. Often we will be in broad agreement with one and disagree with the other, so we find ourselves cheering on our champion and hoping for a knockout punch that will deal with our opponent. How hard it is, though, to say to ourselves, 'Well, I agree with this speaker, so I don't need to listen to her. The person I really need to listen to is my opponent, so that I can understand where he is coming from.' The real risk of this is that I might have to change, and that can generate quite a bit of insecurity.

Jean Vanier says that it is the people I find hard to like who are the ones who can help me most to grow, and growing involves change, sometimes radical change. We like the idea of growing, but only as long as it doesn't inconvenience or disturb us. Listening to those who are different from us, whom we don't like or with whom we disagree, is not an easy task. It engages all kinds of insecurities and yet, paradoxically, it could be one of the most healing things we could do.

I learned a lesson as a young curate that has helped me greatly in later life. I was working at St Andrew's Church, High Wycombe, a thriving charismatic evangelical church and part of a large team ministry made up of all the Anglican churches of the town. Within the team, there was just about every shade of churchmanship. The clergy of the team had a shared communion service, breakfast and meeting every Monday morning, and it was there that I was lifted out of my rather unadventurous evangelical mindset into a world of clergy who were all older and more capable than me, compared to whom I felt quite naïve. Nevertheless, I was made to feel very much at home. It was an excellent team, and it wasn't long before I found a place of safety there. I remember one occasion when one of my colleagues was leading a discussion on death and funerals (it's the kind of thing that we clergy get excited about), and he said, with strong feeling, 'I couldn't live my Christian life without praying for the dead.' An evangelical 'warning buzzer' that I had somehow acquired earlier in my life went off in my head, and I mentally pulled away from the group, leaving it to others to enter into the debate.

When I got home, I decided to listen to myself more deeply. What was going on? Why had my colleague's comment disturbed me so much? And why did I instinctively reach for a kind of theological revolver, ready to fire back if necessary? Part of the story, I discovered as I listened to myself, was an anxiety about conflict, but another part of it was to do with realizing that there was a bit of me saying, 'That view of the dead actually sounds quite interesting.' It was a voice initially submerged by a louder voice that felt obliged to defend traditional evangelical values. As I sensed what was happening, instead of closing down on the subject and checking out 'correct' arguments, I mentally chewed over this strange and in some ways offensive (to me) thought of people praying for the dead.

Eventually my thinking emerged as a little book called *The Quick and the Dead*, and another book that I co-authored with Russ Parker, now called *Healing Death's Wounds*.[12] Both books looked at the theme from an evangelical point of view, but tried to help people to deepen their thinking and experience about the subject. I received a lot of letters as a result of these books, and the ones that moved me most were from evangelicals who wrote along the lines of, 'Thank you for helping me to find a way of loving my loved one who has died'. If you are now thinking 'Is he into spiritualism?' you will just have to read the book to find out that I'm not!

Since that experience, I have cherished this principle—to stop, pause and listen whenever a challenging thought comes my way. I don't always change my views, but I do feel I have been growing as a person. I have taken some of this thinking into a course developed by Acorn, called *Listening to Difference*. In the course, people are given a process of listening to themselves in the presence of someone who is different. I always enjoying leading this workshop, especially when we ask people to share their experience of learning from people who are different from themselves.

There is usually one point in the workshop where someone introduces a question that vexes them. It usually comes when I have been presenting a process that helps people to listen to what is happening in themselves when they are with someone who is disturbingly different from them. After we have been through the process, someone will usually say, 'Surely by listening to this person with an opposite view, you are affirming their view? And if they are wrong, then you are affirming heresy. Furthermore, if you give them the space to express their views, then their wrong thinking will be widely released, infecting others in the room.' I tend to find exactly the same question rising in me. If I give someone with whom I disagree too much space, it will only affirm them and their position.

The only reasonable course of action seems to be to shout back and shut the other person up. This is what has happened between Protestant and Catholic in Northern Ireland, between opposing groups in the homosexuals debate and, more widely, between Western Christian and Middle Eastern Muslim. The fact is that Jesus has called Christian people to love the enemy—to show *agapé* to the person with whom they profoundly disagree. Was Jesus being too idealistic? Surely if we went around loving all our enemies, then our enemies would be vindicated and we would be destroyed?

Let's take a very topical subject—the debate in the church about homosexuality. Supposing you are someone who takes a conservative view on the subject generally and you are in a conversation where a liberal view is being expressed about how the Church should bless same-sex unions. As the conversation proceeds, you listen to your 'enemy' and you become aware of strong feelings welling inside. You believe profoundly that they are wrong, that they must be stopped before they spread their views to more vulnerable listeners who might be corrupted by what you consider wrong teaching. What do you do? You try to stay calm, because you are a Christian and Christians are not meant to say nasty things, but you are aware that you feel angry with this 'enemy'. You partly listen to their arguments, but you also have your own supply of arguments to hand—ones you sincerely believe and have carefully considered. Rather than actually listening to what the other is saying, you focus on working out how you will present the counter-argument. The moment they draw breath, you leap in with your view and, of course, they do exactly what you did while they were speaking. They are mentally rehearsing the arguments, waiting for you to stop so that they can have a turn again. This dynamic often takes place between people with opposing views. Very little 'loving of the enemy' goes on.

How would a listening approach be different? A listening approach would require the listener to take a risk. Rather than rehearsing our arguments, we stop and listen to our opponent. Strange things can happen when this takes place. For a start, it is often the case that the opponent isn't actually being as offensive as we imagined them to be. When they start their argument, we can easily make assumptions about them, based on previous experiences, what we have heard others say about them, and sheer prejudice.

What can also happen, however, is that we actually start to meet the person rather than the argument. This is a major breakthrough. From our point of view, this person may be the 'enemy', but the fact is that they are a fellow human who is worthy of respect. Once we meet the person, we will find it easier to listen to the argument.

Then another, more disturbing thing may happen—something we may even dread happening. We may discover that some aspects of what they are saying sound more right than our arguments. This is a crisis point, when we may well engage our fears and say, 'Aha, I thought so! This is precisely why I mustn't listen to this person. I'm being corrupted!' Sadly, this is not a completely groundless fear, as there are too many stories of vulnerable people being corrupted by manipulative characters. Acknowledging the fear is often enough, however. We don't need to fight back immediately. If we are committed to finding the truth over and above hammering home our point of view, we must be open to the possibility that the person with the opposing view may nevertheless know some aspects of the truth that I need to hear.

In the case of the debate about same-sex unions used as an example above, a listening approach would mean that, by the end of the discussion, both parties would have a clear understanding of the other's beliefs. They would no longer make judgments from knee-jerk reactions based on fears or prejudices. They would have met the person rather than simply encountering the principle. They will probably not have reached a place of agreement, but they will have taken an important step towards loving their enemy, and together they may have discovered more aspects of the truth.

In this context, the emotion that disables me most is fear. All kinds of fears rumble around inside when I am with someone who is different—fears about losing truths that I hold dear; fears about being in angry conflict with another person. I don't think I'm alone in discovering such fears, but I am learning from those who are more courageous than me in facing their fears.

A 1990s film that deeply impressed me was *The Sixth Sense*, in which Bruce Willis takes the role of Dr Malcolm Crowe, a child psychologist. The film is impressive not least for the quality of listening demonstrated by the psychologist, who listens to a young boy, Cole Sear, profoundly troubled because he has vivid encounters with ghosts. Viewers of the film are treated to good Hollywood moments of screeching music and terrifying ghostly appearances.

The young boy feels utterly powerless because of these dreadful experiences, until Dr Crowe urges him to listen to them to discover what they want to say to him. The thought of actually engaging with these dead creatures is too much for Cole at first, but one night, when a ghost appears yet again in his bedroom, he plucks up courage to speak to it. This is the turning point of the film. Sure enough, the ghost is trying to convey something that needs to be heard but, more importantly, Cole begins a journey of healing, having faced his fear and listened to it. By the end of the film, he is still seeing ghosts, but they no longer have power over him. Listening to our fears is never easy. It sometimes takes immense courage, and often the companionship of a good listener.

LISTENING AND EVANGELISM

As Christians we are entrusted with the wonderful privilege of proclaiming the good news of Jesus Christ. We are bearers of good news in a world that is too full of bad news. Unfortunately, we often fail to proclaim the good news as clearly as we might, because we have not listened first. Turning again to Dietrich Bonhoeffer, we read, 'Christians have forgotten that the ministry of listening has been committed to them by him who is himself the great listener and whose work they should share. We should listen with the ears of God that we may speak the Word of God.'[13]

We need to develop the 'evangelistic ear' demonstrated so beautifully in the life of Jesus. The well-known story of the woman at the well of Samaria in John 4 illustrates this clearly. Jesus speaks the word of God to her after listening to her with the ears of God. The compassionate Father in Jesus asks questions of her, and hears her deep longings, her spiritual thirst, her broken relationships. Jesus doesn't roll off some neat impersonal summary of the gospel. He enters into a touching dialogue with her. After listening, he speaks, and is able to apply the precise bit of the good news that the woman needs to hear. The climax of the story is the woman sharing her ultimate dream—'When the Messiah comes, he will proclaim all things to us', to which Jesus answers, 'I am he, the one who is speaking to you' (v. 26). She has no doubt that this is true. Because he has listened to her so lovingly, she is able to receive all that he says to her.

Some years ago, the well-known Pentecostal theologian Walter Hollenweger wrote a daring article in the *Journal of Pentecostal Studies* entitled 'Evangelism: A Non-Colonial Model'.[14] In this article he criticizes what he calls 'colonial evangelism', whereby the evangelist takes his or her culturally conditioned interpretation of the gospel to be the gospel for everybody else. He commends a more Celtic, listening approach, which listens deeply to the culture and then shares the gospel in appropriate ways. He writes:

'Power evangelism'—if such a term is allowed—meant for the early Christians not psychological massage but exposing the truth of the gospel and letting the people discover for themselves what the implications were. Biblical evangelism was thoroughly dialogical and situational. Take the example of Jesus. To the pagan woman who asked him to heal her daughter he replied in the style of his time: 'I am only sent to the children of Israel. One does not take the bread from the table of the children and throw it to the dogs.' And the woman replied: 'Yes, true, but the dogs eat the crumbs which fall from their master's table.' That touched the heart of Jesus. He was able to give up his culturally conditioned racist attitude. He learned something about the gospel from a pagan woman, namely that his gospel was not restricted to the Jews. If Jesus, the Son of God, could learn something from those whom he was evangelizing, can we too not learn something from 'the sinners'?[15]

I am sure some would argue with Professor Hollenweger about this point, but he certainly offers an interesting insight that Jesus modelled a form of evangelism that involves dialogue in which a pagan might actually change the view of the Christian. Historically we have not seen many examples of this. Suddenly those fears arise in us again: 'Well, if we had let pagans set the agenda, all we would have would be a syncretistic mish-mash and we would have completely lost sight of the gospel.' Not quite, because Jesus promised that the Spirit of God would lead us into all truth (John 16:13). If the pagan woman had said, 'Yes, true, but the dogs are powerful enough to savage the children and will do so if the children don't give them some food soon', Jesus would have responded differently, because her comments would have been fundamentally false.

The fact is that Jesus' spirit was totally attuned to discovering truth and distinguishing it from falsehood. He was 'in the Spirit', and if we are in the Spirit we will discern the truth through whatever means it comes to us. Jesus discerned truth in the woman's comments and responded enthusiastically. This is not a sell-out to a lowest-common-denominator approach, in which we all end up vaguely agreeing with each other. It is a commitment to adventure, whereby we are explorers proclaiming loud and clear what we have discovered so far, but always on the look-out for something more.

This approach makes us far more respectful of the person with whom we are sharing the gospel. We should already have the deepest respect for them as fellow humans made in the image of God but, as we share the good news with them, we acknowledge that they may also show us new insights about the kingdom of God. We are listening, therefore, not only to the person's story but also for those bits of wisdom that this particular made-in-the-image-of-God person may have discovered in their life.

I learned an important lesson when I visited Kenya in the mid 1990s. I was taking part in a conference on evangelism. Before the start of the conference, I journeyed to Eldama Ravine to meet up with a good friend of mine, Benjamin Muhalya. It was wonderful to see him again after many years. Ben is an Anglican vicar, and he was leading a church in this beautiful yet poverty-stricken part of Kenya. He was seeing some lively growth through his faithful, gentle ministry. On my second day there, I walked out into fields just beyond his house and gazed at the scene of majestic African beauty that greeted me. I gazed at the far-off mountains and wide open spaces, until my reverie was brought to an abrupt halt. In a nearby village, a travelling evangelist had set up a mission tent and he had now started to preach, using a booming amplification system that rocked me out of my place of stillness. The sermon thundered across the fields, and as I listened I heard the voice urging the people to give money. The discrepancy of an appeal for money in this poor rural area of Africa was more than I could bear and I hurried back to the safety of Ben's house. (See Appendix 1 for the poem *Eldama*, written following this experience.)

I then journeyed on to Kajiado, a small town in Masai country. Here I was involved in speaking at a mission, a wonderful week in which hundreds came from all over Kenya. I felt much enriched by their company, although I was rather less thrilled by an epidemic of scorpions that had come to the surface following recent rain. One of my co-speakers was a man from Australia who had been trained in a preaching school that evidently coached its students in the art of screaming. In normal conversation, my colleague spoke like a reasonable man but, once let loose on the stage, he yelled at the top of his voice as if every tiny point had to be forced home by sheer volume. He spoke at an open-air rally one afternoon, and I watched his sweating face bellowing at the rather nonplussed passers-by, the Masai men and women in the audience looking on politely but clearly somewhat unconvinced.

During the week, I got to know a very wise Kenyan evangelist called Teddy. He was quietly spoken, so one day I asked his opinion on the other preacher: 'When this man preaches he screams at the top of his voice, but your style is much quieter. Which appeals more to Masai culture?' I asked not just because I was growing uncomfortable with my yelling colleague's style, but also because if shouting really was the culturally acceptable way of communication here, then I probably needed explore ways of revving up my talks a bit!

Teddy's answer to my question disturbed me. Very simply he said, 'Preachers do this because they think it is the American style. People see this style linked to money. America is wealthy, and American evangelists, who visit here, preach like this and they look like they have money—indeed they often give generously. So our young men, when they learn to be evangelists, will learn how to preach like this. They hope it will make them successful and, to be honest, wealthy as well.'

I was quite taken aback by such an honest criticism of a preaching style that seemed to be *de rigueur* in this part of the world. So I went on and asked Teddy what his style was. 'My style is different', he told me, 'and not everyone agrees with it. I know the Masai well, and I know they won't listen to a preacher who just arrives, throws a sermon at them and leaves. They are a travelling people, so they will only listen to someone who is prepared to travel with them. I will join them in one of their journeys, and travel with them for several days, and I listen to their stories before I tell mine.

'Just last week I was on such a journey. After a few days walking, we all stopped because one of the Masai had lost a sheep, so we waited while he went and looked for it. We waited for a day, and eventually he came back to us with his sheep, which he carried over his shoulders. As we had a meal together that evening, I told them the story of Jesus and the lost sheep. After I told this story, they smiled, and the man who had gone to find his sheep said, "So your Jesus is a Masai." Once they saw this, they wanted to know much more about him, and for the next few days I told them all about Jesus the Masai.'

Teddy taught me a lesson on evangelism that I will never forget— that every culture we evangelize is known to Jesus. Just because we know him in our home culture, this does not mean that it is his natural culture. The Word became flesh, not British. It is very encouraging to see that much work is being done today on cross-cultural evangelism, with the general ethos being respect of local culture rather than criticism of it. As we evangelize others of a different culture, our first task is to listen deeply to that culture, and then to find words that are understandable to them. This is Bonhoeffer's discipline of listening with the ears of God before we speak the word of God.

AIDAN—A MAN FOR OUR TIMES

One of my favourite places on earth is Lindisfarne, and one of my favourite places on this holy island is the 11-foot-high statue of the 7th-century saint Aidan that stands near the church. No one knows, of course, if the statue is a true likeness of Aidan, but what I like is how well the sculptor, Kathleen Parbury, has depicted the balance of the pastoral and the evangelistic that was so evident in Aidan's life and ministry. He stands with his head slightly raised to heaven, yet not so much as to be of no earthly use! His plain robes speak of simplicity and closeness to the people and culture of his time. Behind him is the cross of Christ, of which he spoke so eloquently. In his left hand he holds up a torch—the flame of the gospel—and this is fitting for Aidan because his name in his native Irish meant 'bright light'. He carried the bright light of the gospel to the un-evangelized people of Northumbria, and he lived it. But the torch is not the only thing he is holding. With his right hand he holds a pastoral staff, which he pulls to his chest as if holding it close to his heart. Here is a man of the cross, who boldly carries the shining gospel message and who also has a great heart for people.

Aidan was a young Irish monk, training at the monastery of Iona founded by the great St Columba. When the Northumbrian king was converted to Christianity, he asked Iona to send an evangelist to his people. Initially they sent Corman, who was, we are told by the Venerable Bede, 'a man of austere disposition', and it seems that in terms of style and approach he was something like my fellow preacher in Kenya. He felt that his task was to 'give it to them', and give it to them strong. He made no headway whatsoever, and returned to Iona complaining about the 'barbarous and obstinate' English. As this was discussed at Iona, Aidan heard the report, and it was he who suggested that what the English needed was an altogether more gentle approach that started by giving people spiritual milk rather than strong meat. Working on that well-tried and tested model of 'he who makes the suggestion gets the job',

Aidan found himself duly commissioned to try his hand at evangelizing the English. Thus it was that, in 635, he was consecrated a bishop and sent to Northumbria, where he made his mission base the island of Lindisfarne.

Aidan's ministry was hugely successful, and I can't help feeling that part of the reason was that Aidan approached the English with a high degree of respect not only for their culture but for each person as an individual. Bede does not give us many stories about Aidan, but those he does tell show us that Aidan was manifestly a man of the Spirit who was a most competent evangelist and Christian leader. He clearly had a great love for people, regardless of their social status, gender, culture or personality. Bede makes a couple of interesting statements about Aidan: 'He was a man of outstanding gentleness, holiness and moderation'[16] and 'He was particularly endowed with the grace of discretion'.[17]

Aidan was not alone in being someone who was clearly holy: many of the early evangelists that we read about lived very close to God and lived exemplary lives. What is more unusual is to find someone commended for their gifts of gentleness, moderation and discretion, which are very much 'listening' qualities. Gentleness and moderation are all to do with being non-imposing, non-colonial, deeply respecting, treating others carefully, moderating our own mood and reaction to give space to the other. The word 'discretion' speaks of carefulness, fair judgment, diplomacy and tact. It is a word that brings together both love and wisdom.

Aidan stands as a model for evangelism in our culture today. Our society will no longer tolerate aggressive or authoritarian forms of evangelism. We cannot go up to people and demand that they put their faith in God. While this may be true, people simply will not be able to hear us. In our evangelism, we need to follow the example of Aidan and listen with the ears of God before we speak the word of God.

Encouragingly, styles of evangelism and mission in Britain are changing. Churches feel a new confidence in the gospel and more Christians are discovering that we really do have some good news to share with a struggling world. There is also a move to a style of evangelism that is altogether more respectful, listening and gentle. The Aidan way is returning—not wholesale, but in significant measure in many expressions of mission today. The listening ethos is becoming a fundamental part of mission, and for me this is a real source of hope. We have become a little less afraid of listening to those who are spiritually different from us; we are choosing to leave our places of safety and encounter the unknown. The rewards, both personally and for the kingdom of God, could be very rich indeed.

THE SPEAKER (4)

The Speaker was irritated. He was thousands of miles away from his office, and he had no way of contacting his colleagues. There was no reception on his mobile phone, and anyway the charger was in his suitcase, and his suitcase was in a lost property office in some unknown part of the world. He had only English money in his wallet and desperately needed to get some local currency. He had come to inspect an AIDS project, but his host had gone off visiting the bereaved.

He sat in a low armchair, with well-worn wooden arms and stuffing protruding from the plastic cover. Leaning back, he did something he had not done for years: he did nothing, for there was nothing to do. He heard the sound of Martha doing some washing in the yard, and some people talking in the distance. It felt peaceful and he dozed quietly.

'I am sorry to disturb you.' The Speaker heard Nkani's voice and for a few moments he wondered where he was. 'You must be tired, you have travelled a long way.'

'Yes. I'm sorry, Nkani, I...' The Speaker got up and felt embarrassed that he had been literally caught napping—something he could never do in the office. Then he remembered.

'I'm very sorry, Nkani, about your friend.'

'He is with Jesus,' said Nkani, and something about the way he said it made the Speaker feel that he really believed it. The Speaker had not been to church for years, but when he was last there, he had felt that all the other people in the place had a matter-of-fact faith. They went to a service, they lived out its rituals, they said their prayers, and they went home. The Speaker had decided that he did not want to do that any more, and he stopped going. Nobody said anything about him no longer going, and he felt angry that they said nothing. For a moment, he felt something of that anger flicker across his soul, but then he saw Nkani looking out of the window at the hills.

'One day there will be a new heaven and a new earth,' said Nkani, and then turned to the Speaker. 'Do you think it will be as beautiful as this earth?'

'I've not really thought,' said the Speaker, and realized that his comment sounded very hollow.

'Mosha loved this world,' said Nkani, now settling himself at the table and pulling a banana from a simple pottery bowl. 'He really loved it. He was a bit younger than me, and not married. He was free.' Nkani smiled a mischievous grin.

'It is why he went to the city. For some reason he thought it would be more exciting, more alive than our world here. I think for a time he found that it was, but then he became very lonely. So many men go to the cities to find work, and they get lonely. Like many lonely men in the cities, Mosha slept with a prostitute. He told me all about it because we are... were best friends.

'He thought I wouldn't want to be his friend any more. He felt very ashamed. It was strange, though, because it was as if doing that thing suddenly made him realize what it meant to live. I mean, he discovered that living was not about making money in the city. It was when he was in the city that he found out how important home was, and so he came home. He feared that his father would be very angry.'

'I'm not surprised,' said the Speaker, but the look on Nkani's face made him wish he hadn't.

'You have not met his father,' replied Nkani gently. 'He is a man of a great heart.'

There was a long pause as Nkani took a bite of the banana and looked out of the window. He seemed to be looking at something with great interest. The Speaker started to feel rather uncomfortable, so he broke the silence with 'And I presume Mosha discovered that he was HIV positive.'

Nkani broke his gaze away from the far distance and looked back at the Speaker. 'Yes. Actually, I think he knew straight away, but he was too afraid to get it checked. He wasn't ill for a while. He only became ill a few months ago.'

The silence that was comfortable to Nkani but not to the Speaker settled again in the warm home. After a while, the Speaker needed to break the silence again, asking, 'If you don't mind the question, what does your name mean?'

Nkani smiled. 'It is short for uNkaniso, which means "bright light".'

'That's nice,' said the Speaker, and wished that his response did not sound so feeble.

'My mother heard God speak to her when she was carrying me,' said Nkani. 'He said to her that the child she was carrying would be a bright light, because there would be a time when the world would be darkened by a terrible disease. He told her that the disease would cause great suffering, but that her child would be one who would share the light of Jesus and bring comfort and healing.

'Amazing, isn't it, that God should tell her that? It was long before anyone here had heard of AIDS.'

'Yes, Nkani, that is amazing,' said the Speaker, and he really did think it was amazing. 'I am sure you are a bright light here.'

Nkani smiled modestly. 'I try to be like a mirror. I am not the light. He is the light. But if I can keep my mirror polished and turn it gently to those who are in darkness, then I think they may find him and be comforted.'

'Well, I'm sure many are very comforted by you, Nkani. Now I'm wondering about my luggage. Do you think we could phone the airport again? There are many things in my case that I need.'

'How dark is this disease?' asked Nkani, looking very serious and completely disregarding the Speaker's request.

The Speaker became aware of all his research and studies on the subject of this hideous sickness. When he first encountered it, he had been appalled. Now he had become accustomed to it, and it had become an academic subject for him. When he saw the intensity in Nkani's face, however, it evoked the feelings that had besieged him in those early days. 'It is very dark, Nkani. It is very dark indeed.'

'Then the light has to be very bright indeed. I am so glad you have come. This is your home while you are here, and while you are in this home, you will help polish my mirror. I have not been shining bright enough. Thank you so much for coming.'

For reasons the Speaker could not understand, he felt a strong emotion in the base of his throat. He wanted to speak, to say something, to respond, but he could think of no words that described how he felt. He became conscious that he was rubbing the wooden arms of the chair and looking intently at Nkani. He then realized what the emotion was. He felt valued. Someone actually valued him, not because he had useful knowledge, but because he was who he was.

The feeling was becoming too strong, so to stop it he finally found words and said, 'Well, are you going to show me around your village?'

'Of course,' said Nkani, and his white teeth shone radiantly from his gentle smile.

Chapter 5

TO GAIN WISDOM

There is so much knowledge,
Expertise and confidence;
All we need now is
To gain wisdom.

A few months ago, I reached a landmark birthday. Now, even as I am about to tell you which landmark it is, I feel anxious! From the age of 30 onwards, the decades bring anxieties related to Western society's perceptions about how people are valued. Whenever we switch our TVs to one of the commercial stations, we usually see some wrinkle-free lovely, telling us what secret potion she has used to stave off the horrifying effects of ageing. Well, I'll own up and tell you that I've reached 50, where that wrinkling and greying process accelerates to confirm the truth that you have been trying to avoid for ten years, which is that you are well and truly middle-aged.

As I approached this great event, I was comforted by those kind friends who said, 'You don't look anything near 50', and I found myself feeling particularly fond of the *young* person who thought I was under 40. Of course, as a humble and saintly Christian, I chased such proud thoughts well away from me… I wish. But it did get me thinking. Almost the entire content of the remarks about my age related to exterior appearance. Why was it that no one came up to me to say, 'Goodness, are you 50? Well, judging by your wisdom, I would guess you were at least 60.' As a Western society, we are obsessed with the appearance. The cult of celebrity only enforces this obsession, as magazines take photos with deft use of lighting and airbrushing to make our heroes look years younger than they actually are.

For my birthday, then, I wanted to celebrate wisdom. I don't particularly enjoy the effects of ageing on my body, but I do love the growth of the inner life that I see, admittedly more easily in my friends than I do in myself. As I approached 50, I kept on thinking to myself, 'That's really quite a few years of experience and accumulated wisdom.' My birthday celebration consisted of going out for a meal with my wife and several friends. When I invited them, I asked if they would bring, as a gift, a word of wisdom— some treasure that they had discovered during their years here on earth, that they could share with me. The result was wonderful. As the meal progressed, each person opened a card and read out a wise saying that was precious to them, or narrated a story, or explained a particular Bible verse that meant so much to them. There was a happy mixture of both serious and comic. By the end of the evening, I felt I was taking home a treasure trove.

Despite the obsession with appearance in today's culture in the West, we do get signs that the human spirit still longs for wisdom. Among the films that have been hugely popular in recent years are the *Star Wars* films. They are set in a complex world of inter-stellar life, high-speed space vehicles and a multitude of extra-terrestrial life forms, and an ongoing conflict between good and evil. Technology is highly advanced, and part of the thrill of the films for me is see- ing the latest galactic gadgets. Yet, despite this high-tech fest, the planetary environments are quite often primitive: our heroes can be found living in a network of caves, for example, which adds a fascinating dimension to the ethos of the films. It is the resonance of primitive life, a signal of something to do with depth, speaking of ancient things and of wisdom. And the true heroes are the ones like Yoda, who, usually with rather sober, unfeeling faces, share deep nuggets of wisdom that somehow counterbalance the high-tech machine-driven world that we are connecting with.

Another highly popular series of films is the *Lord of the Rings* trilogy. Set in the fantasy realm of Middle Earth, they include no high-tech machinery, but they do fulfil our modern-day need for high drama and action. In the midst of the frantic activity, the travelling and fighting, we have moments of deep stillness, mystery and wisdom. These are often pivotal moments in the film (such as the meeting with Galadriel in Lothlorien), and show how, in Tolkien's mind, wisdom was the driving force of his stories—wisdom that prevails over greed and folly.

Such books and films awaken us to an instinctive need in humans for such wisdom.

FINDING WISDOM

Richard Foster opened his ground-breaking book *Celebration of Discipline* with the following statement: 'Superficiality is the curse of our age. The doctrine of instant satisfaction is a primary spiritual problem. The desperate need today is not for a greater number of intelligent people, or gifted people, but for deep people.[18]

The age he was writing about was the Western world of the 1980s, and the book did much to help Christian people seek disciplines that would help them travel deeper in their spirituality. In general, however, the problem of superficiality has become worse. The desire for instant satisfaction has been exacerbated by our high-tech IT-dominated world. The 1980s and 1990s did not produce noticeably greater numbers of wise people.

Has the Church become wiser in the past 20 years? Has the Church maintained or developed a reputation as a receptacle of wisdom? Sadly, the media image of the Church tends to be quite the opposite. Part of the problem is that the Church, in its often desperate attempts to appear 'relevant', has simply replicated the world's ways of doing things. If King Solomon was a minister in today's Church and two mothers came to him arguing about who was the true parent of a child, the chances are that he would refer them to a committee, a report or a specialist. Perhaps one of our most fervent prayers for our church leaders is that they should be men and women of wisdom.

One of the problems is that to gain wisdom, we need time, and for many of us time is becoming more and more scarce. Some years ago, I had the privilege of visiting the beautiful state of Kerala in South India. I was there for only two weeks, but it was enough to give me a lifelong love for that mysterious, glorious and suffering nation. On one occasion I travelled from Kottayam to Trivandrum— a four-hour train ride, which I spent mostly standing by an open door, watching the passing landscape with fascination. At times we would pass through dusty little shanty towns, and children would run out with delight on their faces and wave at us, perhaps dreaming of a day when they might have the money to ride on a train. We also travelled through marshlands and past many back-waters busy with small fishing boats.

As the sun began to set at the end of another hot day, I saw a small promontory on a lake, covered with candle-light, and a trickle of people making their way to a highly decorated shelter in the middle of the promontory. In this shelter I could make out a seated figure, a wise man. At the end of a weary day, people were making their way to this man to speak to him about a pressing problem or concern, and collect from him a word of wisdom.

As the train took me past this tranquil scene, I felt sad that Christianity has, generally speaking, lost its commitment to seeking wisdom. Can you imagine clergy sitting in little booths outside their churches on Thursday evenings, with local people coming to them for a word of wisdom? Why does the thought seem so humorous to us?

THE WISDOM OF THE DESERT

From the fourth century onwards, the extraordinary renewal movement that took place in the deserts of the Middle East included a strong commitment to wisdom. The mothers and fathers of the desert developed reputations for being deeply wise people. The time they were able to spend seeking God meant that they discovered precious gems of wisdom that could bring great wealth to a Church that was rapidly growing superficial and worldly. People poured out into the deserts to find a wise man or woman to guide them in their Christian life and witness. These pilgrims would follow the example of Jesus, who went out into the wilderness and did battle with Satan, defeating his temptations with quotations from scripture (Luke 4:1–13). The journey out into the desert was part of the challenge. It might take many days to reach the monk or nun. When the pilgrims finally got there, they might have to wait hours, days or even years for a response from the wise man or woman. Wisdom didn't— and doesn't—come cheap. You have to work to find it.

I remember a story about wisdom told by John Finney, at the time the Anglican Officer for the Decade of Evangelism. He told of a young vicar who went on a retreat to a monastery. It was a silent retreat, but at the end of it the retreatants were invited to meet with one of the monks, and this young vicar went for his half-hour appointment. For the first 20 minutes, the monk looked intently at him and said nothing. The vicar felt rather uncomfortable as the monk's eyes seemed to be piercing into his soul. Eventually the monk spoke, and said one sentence about the vicar that reduced him to tears. He wept for the next ten minutes, at the end of which he felt much better. The monk then pronounced a blessing and the vicar left feeling quite transformed.

I found this a fascinating story, revealing the monk's ability to listen to God and to the young vicar, and speak a word of wisdom that was transforming. I am sure that it was a gift that the monk had developed through his own journey into wilderness places.

LISTENING TO THE BUTTERFLIES

We all have wisdom within us. Each time I meet someone, they may give me a gift of wisdom, and I may give them such a gift. How do we find this inner wisdom? I am fairly convinced that wisdom does not come by acquiring a lot of books of wise sayings, although I have caught myself thinking this way at times. Someone says something profound, and I think, 'I like the sound of that; I must use it somewhere'—and there is a sneaky bit of me that hopes others will think me profound for using such a thought. Yes, of course we can share discovered wisdom with others, but we cannot live on borrowed wisdom. We will need to find our own supply.

A few years ago I read *The Diving-Bell and the Butterfly* by Jean-Dominique Bauby. He had been editor of the French magazine *Elle*, when he had a massive stroke that left him completely paralysed. He was left able to move only one eyelid, as he was suffering the rare condition described starkly as 'locked-in syndrome'. Remarkably, he used this one movement to communicate with people, and in time he was even able to dictate the book about his experience.

The title of the book provides the images for his contrasting experiences of this terrible trauma. The image of the diving-bell describes how it felt to be trapped in an unmoving body. It was as if he was in a diving-bell at the bottom of the ocean, utterly dependent on others for every detail of his life. He tells with great frustration how he longed to hug his two children, and how he was denied the most basic freedoms that most of us enjoy—watching a football match on the TV, for example, only for a nurse to switch it off before the end. He had no way of stopping her. The sheer helplessness of his situation was frightening even to read about. At the same time, he was also able to use the analogy of the butterfly to describe his situation. In one chapter he describes one of the effects of his illness, which was that one ear became deaf while the other amplified all sounds. Thus, there were times when everyday sounds were agonizingly loud, and he would long for quietness:

Far from such din, when blessed silence returns, I can listen to the butterflies inside my head. To hear them, one must be calm and pay close attention, for their wingbeats are barely audible. Loud breathing is enough to drown them out. This is astonishing: my hearing does not improve, yet I hear them better and better. I must have the ear of the butterfly.[19]

The experience of being 'locked in' led him to explore his own soul. As a result, he discovered pockets of wisdom he never knew were there. Bauby's story tells us that even if the unimaginable should happen and we end up completely trapped in some way, we can still seek out the interior places of our soul:

My cocoon becomes less oppressive, and my mind takes flight like a butterfly. There is so much to do. You can wander off in space or in time, set out for Tierra del Fuego or for King Midas's court. You can visit the woman you love, slide down beside her and stroke her still-sleeping face. You can build castles in Spain, steal the Golden Fleece, discover Atlantis, realize your childhood dreams and adult ambitions.[20]

God has created humans with extraordinary depths and reserves but, sadly, we seldom encounter these depths unless we are faced with a crisis or a time of suffering. The Gospel stories show us that Jesus was familiar with the deep places of his heart. I don't think this made him a terribly intense kind of person, and I am sure that it is not his intention for us all to live in such a way that every word we utter is of profound significance. God forbid! What Jesus demonstrated, though, was knowing where to find resources of wisdom when he needed them. He listened to his own heart, he listened to others and he listened to his Father in heaven. This three-dimensional listening meant that he regularly offered wisdom that was quite different from the wisdom of the day, and often exposed the latter's superficial nature.

Take the example of the woman caught in adultery as recounted by John (John 8:3–11). One day, the scribes and the Pharisees come to Jesus, dragging with them a woman whom they claim has been caught in the act of adultery. They remind Jesus that the law of Moses is very clear on this subject: the woman should be taken out and stoned to death. John tells us that they did this to test

Jesus, 'so that they might have some charge to bring against him' (v. 6).

The Pharisees had thought hard about this and felt sure that they were going to trick Jesus successfully. On the one hand, if he followed the law strictly, then he must allow them to stone the woman. Then his reputation for love and mercy would be completely ruined, and he could no longer be called a friend of sinners. Furthermore, it would bring Jesus into direct conflict with the Romans, who did not allow non-Romans to carry out the death penalty. On the other hand, if Jesus pardoned the woman, it would look as if he was encouraging a lax approach to the law of Moses, and that he was condoning, even encouraging, people to commit adultery. The Pharisees would have been delighted at this dilemma. Surely this would trap Jesus! But it didn't, and the reason it didn't was because of his wisdom.

The men made their accusation, and then it was over to Jesus. Few could have guessed what he did next. He bent down to the ground, and wrote something in the dust. William Barclay, in his commentary on John, tells us that the evangelist here uses the word *katagraphein* for 'write', which is often used to mean 'write down a record against'. It is quite possible that Jesus actually wrote down the sins of the men who had brought the woman. He might have looked one of the men in the eye, and then written down 'theft' and, for another, 'hurting your wife', and so on. It is a fascinating thought that each of those men might have been presented with a written statement of their own personal sins. If this is the case, then Jesus was listening at a prophetic depth to each of the accusers.

Jesus also listens deeply to the woman. What does he see of her life as he looks at her, listens to her? We don't know, but it is quite likely that he sees a wounded life, a woman like the woman at the well who is longing to be loved, and a woman who at this time and probably many times before, is being badly treated by men. Furthermore, Jesus listens not just to the Pharisees and to the woman. He is also listening to something deep in himself—perhaps a natural compassion for the woman who is being made a scapegoat for the men's sin. Maybe a part of him is attracted to the woman—he is a fully human man, after all. He may also feel anger with these hypocritical men. Perhaps he feels one of his tirades against the Pharisees rising up.

His wisdom leads him to make the best response possible, however. He is quickly aware that the real problem is the hypocrisy of the men. Someone once said that this story should not be known as 'the woman caught in adultery', but 'the men caught in hypocrisy'. So Jesus comes up with this profoundly wise response: 'Let anyone among you who is without sin be the first to throw a stone' (v. 7), and down he goes again to continue writing on the ground.

Now the dilemma is with the Pharisees. They are not men of wisdom, and their foolishness and hypocrisy have been exposed by just one sentence from Jesus, so with much shame they leave the woman and Jesus. Incredibly it is their sin, not the woman's wrongdoing, that has become the focus of the story.

There is one more bit of wisdom given, this time for the woman. Is Jesus now going to condone her adultery, in effect, as if the sin wasn't really important? No, the sin was important, and Jesus makes that clear through his saying, 'From now on do not sin again' v. 11). He is giving the woman another chance. The way he has treated her has inspired her to live differently. Wisdom and love have come together and brought healing and renewal for her. If any of those Pharisees had stopped to think about what was going on, they too would have had a chance for renewal and healing. It is available to all.

BECOMING WISE

One of the best-known verses in the Bible is Proverbs 9:10, which tells us that the fear of the Lord is the beginning of wisdom. Craig Bartholomew, in *Reading Proverbs with Integrity*, writes:

'Fear' should not be understood here as the slavish terror before an evil father or political leader. Fear refers rather to a sense of God as God, as

the eternal creator who is also our redeemer… 'Fear' is thus the appropriate attitude towards God as the holy, gracious one who has rescued us from slavery and made us part of his people, and now calls us to live accordingly.[21]

This kind of fear is about a relationship that is rooted in our human response to God who has rescued us and given us a place of belonging. Far from being a nervous dread of an overbearing and rule-imposing parent, it is more a response of gratitude. It is perhaps the emotion of the prodigal son as he felt the embrace of his father who, through his welcoming love, helped him to find home again. Wisdom, then, like charity, starts at home. It is not a commodity that we pick up from a shop, nor is it a course we can study at a superficial level, nor even a skill to develop. According to Proverbs, it is primarily what happens when we know that we belong in the home of our God.

Jesus knew he was beloved by his Father in heaven, who publicly proclaimed him beloved at his baptism (Luke 3:22). It was from that living, dynamic relationship that he gained wisdom. The beginning of wisdom is therefore in our relationship with God, where we come into his home and find that it is safe to ask him the awkward questions. It is the place where we bring the things that frighten us, disturb us and confuse us, where in quiet listening we discern his voice to us. Of course, we can and do benefit greatly from others who have learned wisdom this way, and write it in books and speak it from pulpits. But to some extent, that will come to us second-hand. Each of us needs to learn the discipline of the fear of the Lord, whereby we give time to listening to God for his wise word for us. This can be done personally, or with the help of a safe friend such as a spiritual director.

The key point at this stage is that we should learn to journey more deeply along the path of wisdom as we listen to others, to our hearts and to God, which is the subject of the next chapter.

The Good News Bible version of Proverbs 18:13 reads, 'Listen before you answer. If you don't, you are being stupid and insulting.'

Our Western world places great value on knowledge and expertise, so we are often eager to share these things with others. It makes us feel more confident. The problem is that our very lack of confidence means that we often offer our knowledge and expertise before we have truly listened. By learning to listen, we can add wisdom to our knowledge and expertise and, in so doing, not only equip minds but touch hearts. 'If any of you is lacking in wisdom,' says James, 'ask God' (James 1:5). Now is the time to be asking.

THE SPEAKER (5)

The Speaker had never heard so much singing. It was not his style. Some of the tunes sounded familiar, but others were most definitely not his style. In the days when he used to go to church, he had preferred the traditional hymns. In fact, it was the vicar bringing his guitar to church that was the last straw. He remembered making some sarcastic comment to the vicar about *Top of the Pops* as he left church that morning, and he was frankly glad of an excuse not to have to go again. It was another source of argument with Caroline. She liked *Top of the Pops* and she liked guitars in church. He felt she only liked them because it annoyed him.

During the three days he had been in Africa, he had caught himself thinking a lot about Caroline. He didn't like it. He thought he had sorted that one out. They had agreed to part. It was amicable; it was efficient. Lots of people in the business world separated. Lots of men at his club were in the same position. It happened. There was nothing to be ashamed of. No other parties were involved. It was decent and in order and the lawyers were handling the financial side quite adequately. It couldn't have gone better. So why did he keep thinking of her?

He stopped himself thinking about Caroline by trying to join in a hymn. It was in Zulu, but he recognized the tune. 'Through all the changing scenes of life'—yes, he knew that one, some of the words at least. 'O make but trial of his love, experience will decide, how blest are they who in his truth confide.' Hmm, his mind was wandering again. Love. He didn't really like that word. These Africans were rather keen on love and rather too emotional with it for his liking.

'Come, meet Father Matthew.' Nkani's soft voice brought the Speaker back out of his mental wanderings. To his embarrassment, he realized that Nkani was holding his hand as they walked across the rough ground to the robed figure. Men were shovelling earth into Mosha's grave, while others sang and women wept.

Father Matthew smiled a broad grin, not quite what the Speaker expected at a funeral. 'Nkani and Martha have told me much about you. It is very special for us to have you with us.'

The Speaker found himself thinking, 'Yes, you must be feeling honoured to have an international speaker in your humble village', but he quickly stopped that voice, not because he disagreed with it but because the vicar was saying something else. '...and so young,' he said. The Speaker assumed he was speaking about Mosha.

'Yes, I am sorry,' he said and they all laughed. He suddenly felt very awkward. Who had the vicar been talking about?

'I am sorry—it is probably my accent. English is my second language.' The Speaker never did find out what he had said. He didn't have the confidence to ask anyone. He hated looking foolish. And yet he was.

Mosha had lived in a beautifully crafted round mud-walled house with a thatched roof, and the funeral party gathered in the house and in the area of ground surrounding it. The sun felt hot, but nonetheless the cup of tea was welcome. The Speaker was the only white man present, and the children kept coming up to him and smiling and studying him.

He felt most uncomfortable. He wanted to leave but he had none of his usual props. He could plead no important meeting to attend, no train to catch. His mobile phone could not go off. He was stuck in the midst of this group of mourners who mostly spoke in Zulu and drank tea that was terribly sweet and ate cake that was too dry.

'Do you have a wife and family?' a voice next to him asked. It was Father Matthew again. He had taken his robes off and he was wearing some very worn grey trousers and a black clerical shirt that was too tight, with a torn sleeve. Why did he have to ask about his wife and family? It was not a subject the Speaker wanted to discuss.

'Yes—a wife,' replied the Speaker abruptly. Well, technically they were not divorced yet.

'Then you are blessed,' replied Father Matthew.

'I suppose, as a priest, you are not allowed to marry.'

Father Matthew laughed again and the Speaker noticed that

several teeth were missing. 'No, no—I am an Anglican priest. We are allowed to marry. I was married to Miriam, but she is now with the Lord.' Another death, another grief. The Speaker was starting to feel tired with death. He had no language to respond to this grief.

'But you are no longer with your wife,' said Father Matthew.

'How did you know that?' snapped the Speaker. 'Who told you? No one here knows that.'

'Your face told me. Do not be ashamed.'

'I am not ashamed,' said the Speaker, downing the last bit of tea, which was full of leaves that got caught in his throat and made him cough, irritating him even more. Father Matthew slapped him on the back and then said, 'My brother, I was married. I loved Miriam. I loved her so much, and she loved me so much. But we had our arguments like many couples. She had quite a temper! Then she died and for a long time I felt lost. I see that lostness in you. The difference is that I cannot get my wife back. You can.'

This was all getting far too personal for the Speaker. Anglican vicars that he had met in the past did not pry into other people's business like this one did. He really did not want to be drawn out on the subject. 'It really is something I would rather not talk about,' he muttered, hoping that would be the end of it.

'I know. It is none of my business. My brother, if love has gone completely cold, then it may not be rekindled. I know this happens. But I see embers in your heart, and I think an African breeze is blowing upon them. Don't underestimate the effects of the African breeze on your soul. Thank you so much for coming today. We feel very honoured.' And with that he went into the house to see Mosha's family.

The Speaker was left holding his empty teacup. The sun was still hot on his back, but a refreshing wind was blowing from the mountains. He stood for many moments gazing at the contours of the distant peaks. A strange mood came over him. It was loneliness, yet comfort. It was vulnerability, yet safety. It was disturbance, yet peace. He understood none of it. He suddenly noticed Nkani and felt oddly rescued, so he said, 'Oh Nkani, there you are. Now, about finding a bank…'

'Yes, my friend,' said Nkani with such kindness, and the Speaker noticed his red eyes and shiny cheeks, still moist with tears of grief. The Speaker said quickly, 'It can wait' and, to his surprise, found that he had put a hand on Nkani's shoulder.

Chapter 6

TO TOUCH HEAVEN

*The human spirit
Has never survived on bread alone.
There is a longing in us all
To touch heaven.*

My elderly father died at the beginning of 2003. His spiritual life was nurtured mostly on a diet of fairly traditional Anglican spirituality. He was not comfortable with either the 'paraphernalia' (as he called it) of the Anglo-catholics, nor the 'over-emotionalism' of the charismatics. We had many a lively discussion over a glass of wine, and even when he was well into his 90s he would put forward his own opinions about the Anglican church with some force. Just occasionally the conversation would become more personal, and something of the roots of both his faith and his doubts emerged. From time to time he would speak about the afterlife, as he called it, but sadly he always spoke about it with some anxiety, fearing that he would not be good enough to enter it. No amount of theological argument about grace could settle him about this. Despite his doubts about his own place there, however, he did have a strong belief in life after death. It was only after he died that I discovered how an experience in his teenage years had awakened him to the reality of paradise.

It was my job to sort through his desk, and among the many little scraps of paper, shopping lists, ancient Christmas cards and reams of old carbon copy paper, I came across some pages in his handwriting that were clearly written relatively recently. They were entitled *Paradise (God's Garden)*. He never kept a journal or engaged in any kind of creative writing, so this piece of work was very unusual. He opens his story thus:

With advancing years I look back and think of times or occasions of great happiness—perhaps even a glimpse of paradise on earth. I am lucky and have had so much happiness in my life, but one simple incident often recurs in my memory.

He then describes his life in his childhood home in Derbyshire. He speaks of this lovely home with a 'long garden and orchard, surrounded by green fields in which cows grazed and hay was made'. He tells us that it was mid-June and he was 17 years old. He attended a boarding school and had come home for summer half-term. On the Saturday evening, he had just enjoyed a meal, and came out into the garden on his own and sat on the old swing.

The evening was perfect summer, warm and still, and the chirping of the birds finding a place to roost; across the fields about a mile away, smoke came up from household chimneys of a small village. In the still of the evening the grind of the trams starting and stopping was very audible. I sat motionless on the swing seat. I was home. I had love, kindness, home-grown strawberries, new potatoes and garden peas for dinner. The sounds, the beauty of the evening, being at home with those I loved so much, the beauty of the hawthorn blossoms and their scent. Was this my earthly paradise? I wonder. The memory of this happiness is still fresh in my mind after more than 70 years. If Paradise is better than this, then its happiness surpasses the comprehension of mankind.

I found myself intensely moved by these words for all kinds of reasons. Among my feelings was the recognition that so many of us have 'numinous' moments, when the curtain dividing this world from paradise seems to lift temporarily. In those moments, we experience a deep contentment, a sense of communion with something far greater than ourselves, a sense of eternity and a totally different perspective on life. These moments of touching heaven will be among our most treasured memories in life, and, as in the case of my father, lose nothing of their quality with the passing of time, because they are beyond time.

As far as I know, my father was not going through a 'religious phase' when he had this experience. He had not just been to a charismatic meeting, nor had he returned from a pilgrimage to Walsingham. He was effectively just going about his normal life, and then suddenly, without any invitation, he encountered paradise. He is not alone in the experience.

F.C. Happold, in his classic work *Mysticism*, includes a chapter in his book that is a collection of such experiences recounted by 'ordinary' people. He introduces these stories thus:

I have argued in this Study of mysticism that mystical experience is not something confined to those who have risen to the heights of Contemplation, but that it can be present in a less developed form in quite ordinary men and women. An experience of the sort, which may, without unjustifiably stretching the meaning of the word, be called mystical, may happen to anyone, sometimes quite unexpectedly; but when it occurs, it is clearly recognizable. It may happen only once in a lifetime; but when it does happen, it brings an illumination and a certainty which can rarely, if ever, be reached by the rational consciousness and may change the whole tenure of life. [22]

David Runcorn, in his book, *Choice, Desire and the Will of God*, writes also about these experiences:

Research has revealed a remarkably high percentage of people with no religious commitment who have received important experiences of sensing 'God', 'divine Spirit', or a 'numinous presence' at moments in their life. What is less well known is that these experiences are on the increase at the very moment that traditional church life is in steep decline. [23]

Recent research was carried out by David Hay at Nottingham University on the spiritual life of those who don't go to church. A survey originally carried out in 1987 was repeated in 2000 using exactly the same questions. Non-churchgoing people were interviewed and, in 1987, 48 per cent testified to some kind of spiritual experience (an awareness of God's presence, the presence of the dead, awareness of evil and so on). By 2000 that figure had risen to 76 per cent. This is a remarkable rate of increase and suggests that our society has become either more aware of the realm of the spirit, or more willing to own up to it. Probably it is a bit of both. The point to ponder is that in today's society three out of four people are having experiences of the spirit. They may have turned their back on institutional Christianity, but they are remarkably open to the Spirit and it seems that they are less shy about owning up to it.

All this points to that ability within each of us to listen to God. All humans have a God-designed tuning system that enables us to become aware of God, of the spiritual world, of 'the other', and of evil. It is sad that when many people join churches, this wonderful facility in our human nature tends not to be encouraged. So much of church life is very cerebral, wordy and ordered, so that there is little opportunity for people either to experience or share these moments of paradise. There was certainly no place in my father's formal experience of church life where he could share that experience of heaven.

LOOKING THROUGH THE GLASS

What we have to develop, and encourage in each other, is the capacity to 'see and see and perceive, to hear and hear and understand', to use the language of Isaiah 6:9. There is a seeing beyond seeing, and a hearing beyond hearing. George Herbert wrote, in his poem 'Elixir':

A man that looks on glass
On it may stay his eye,
But if he pleaseth, through it pass
And then the heaven espy.

We all have that ability to look through the glass and not just at it. My father, all those years ago, might have simply looked at the beautiful view from his swing. Instead he looked through and caught a glimpse of paradise. Something within him was open, warm and receptive. This is a work of the Holy Spirit: he comes to make us more open. 'The Spirit... will guide you into all the truth,' said Jesus to his disciples (John 16:13), and I don't think he was referring simply to Christian doctrine. 'Truth' covers all that is true, and paradise is most true.

One of my favourite examples of this openness is the story of Moses and the burning bush (Exodus 3:1ff.). The episode takes place in the context of the Hebrews' suffering in Egypt, calling out to God to intervene and deliver them. The scene moves from the groaning Israelites to a lost soul in the wilderness. At this stage, Moses is not the great biblical hero that we know he becomes. He is a man who has made a fatal mistake and finds himself literally out in the wilderness. He has become a shepherd in Midian, and day by day he cares for the sheep, leading them to places where they can find some food and refreshment. He frequently passes all kinds of desert shrubs and trees. They are the ordinary stuff of his everyday life.

Then, one day, the ordinary becomes extraordinary. A bush catches alight, but it is not consumed. This is fire, but a different kind of fire. The writer tells us that Moses said, 'I must turn aside and look at this great sight, and see why the bush is not burned up' (Exodus 3:3). The writer then tells us, 'When the Lord saw that he had turned aside to see, God called to him out of the bush, "Moses, Moses!"' (v. 4). This is very significant. God was looking to see if Moses was alert enough to stop his ordinary and important work, to turn aside to look and listen deeply. Moses quickly realizes that the ground has become holy, and he removes his sandals as a sign of respect. He is now vulnerable, open, humble and ready to listen to God. The Lord then gives him the extraordinary instructions that will change the course of history. And it all started with one very ordinary desert bush. Although Moses struggled with the message, he at least demonstrated a willingness to hear God.

A story is told of an atheist and a rabbi. The atheist asked the rabbi, 'Why did God speak to Moses from the thornbush?' The rabbi answered, 'To teach you that there is no place on earth where God's glory is not, not even in a humble thornbush.' In that spectacular vision received by Isaiah, described for us at the beginning of Isaiah 6, the prophet learns from the angels that heaven *and earth* are full of the glory of God. Isaiah would have had no problem believing that heaven was full of the glory of God, but could the damaged and fallen things of earth be full of heavenly glory? The answer is emphatically 'yes'. There is no place that the glory of God cannot touch. It may be revealed in any part of life—through a momentary look at the sky, through the song of a bird, through the smile of a child, in the shape of a building. Christians can all too easily get into the frame of mind of thinking that God will only ever communicate through something 'spiritual', such as a sermon. But because the whole earth is full of God's glory, anything, however menial, can be the means through which God can speak.

R.S.Thomas caught this story well in his poem, 'The Bright Field',[24] in which he describes the experience of seeing the sun shining in a field. It is an apparently ordinary scene, but he appeals to us to 'turn aside like Moses to the miracle of the lit bush'. Such a scene can be a pearl of great price.

We do find it hard to acknowledge the sacredness of the present moment, to open ourselves to the possibility that it may hold a gift of revelation. In his very influential book on the Holy Spirit, *The Go-between God*, John Taylor, at the time Bishop of Winchester, wrote:

I am writing this book out of a conviction that nothing is more needed by humanity today, and by the church in particular, than a recovery of a sense of 'beyond-ness' in the whole of life, to revive the springs of wonder and of adoration. And oddly enough to our distorted view, our retrieval of mystery is dependent on our reinstatement of the body, with its rhythms and dreams and ways of knowing.[25]

More than 30 years ago, John Taylor was appealing for a recovery of this sense of 'beyondness', and, significantly, he links it with a need not to disregard the material world, but to reinstate it. Our bodies, as indeed all of God's good creation, can be sacramental. Our humanity has the capacity to eat, drink, make love, walk and talk; it can also dream, wonder, see visions and touch heaven. These are not two extremes on a scale, whereby we struggle to get spiritual by denying the material. It is possible to see the extraordinary in the ordinary, heaven in a glass, the angel of God in a desert shrub. One of the ways to do this is to regain our sense of wonder.

In an age of cynicism, it is difficult to wonder. We start to wonder and then we catch ourselves trying to provide a rational answer to the mystery that is captivating us. We look up at the stars in amazement, and we hear the voice of the scientist demoting such wonder to a series of facts. We find ourselves moved to tears by a country and western song, and then hear the voice of someone saying, 'Oh, you don't like that rubbish, do you?' We feel immensely moved at a little scene in a film, and all too quickly hear the critic's voice damning it as 'cheesy'. I am one of the few who actually own up to feeling intensely moved when Captain von Trapp joins in with the children singing 'The hills are alive...' in that touching scene in *The Sound of Music*. In this world, we have to be quite confident to resist cynicism, and this is partly because, when we allow ourselves to experience wonder, we have 'taken off our shoes' as Moses did, and made ourselves vulnerable. Our world is not kind to the vulnerable, yet the rewards of vulnerably approaching the burning bush are very great.

WINDOWS OF THE SOUL

A book I have much enjoyed reading recently is Ken Gire's *Windows of the Soul*. It is subtitled 'Experiencing God in new ways', and Gire has certainly helped me to do just that. He explains his term, 'windows of the soul':

Windows of the soul is a way of seeing that begins with respect. The way we show respect is to give it a second look, a look not of the eyes but of the heart. But often we don't give something a second look because we don't think there is anything there to see.

To respect something is to understand that there is a something there to see, that it is not all surface, that something lies beneath the surface, something that has the power to change the way we think or feel, something that may prove so profound a revelation as to change not only how we look at our lives, but how we live them.[26]

Here is an invitation, to see and look at things at a deeper level. It is Kathleen Raine's 'mountain behind the mountain, knowledge under the leaves'.[27] Ken Gire illustrates this point as he writes about his experience of Vincent Van Gogh's art. He tells of how he visited the Paul Getty Museum in California, which had just purchased Van Gogh's *Irises*. He took a quick look at the picture, made a mumbled complaint about how such an ordinary picture cost such an inordinate amount of money, and went on his way. He then tells how, a few years later, he was in a grocery store and heard Don McLean's song 'Starry, starry night', which is a tribute to Van Gogh —in particular the lyric, 'They would not listen, they did not know how. Perhaps they'll listen now.'

Gire suddenly felt that he was one of those who was failing to listen, and chose to 'listen now'. He discovered that the artist was actually trying to say something through his work, and he had to learn to listen, even if the language was unfamiliar. He decided to start to listen to what Van Gogh was trying to say through his paintings. Over a few pages in his book, he describes what he learned from the great artist and how he grew to love *Irises*, as it was a painting that celebrated Van Gogh's temporary recovery from darkness and madness. In this story, he includes those touching words of the artist, 'There may be a great fire in our soul, yet no one comes to warm himself at it, and the passers-by see only a wisp of smoke coming through the chimney, and go along their way.'[28]

The discovery of Van Gogh and his art was, for Ken Gire, an experience of opening a window in his soul, through which came fresh experiences of hearing God's voice. We are given more opportunities to open windows in our souls than we think. The important thing is to become alert, to give space, and to be expectant.

From time to time we have to stop in life and take stock, especially those of us who travel through life at speed. I love that film, *Speed*, with Keanu Reeves and Sandra Bullock. Throughout the film, our heroes are trapped on a bus that, if it slows to less than 50mph, will trigger a bomb planted by a terrorist. Some of us are a bit like that: we feel compelled to travel through our lives at speed, and fear that if we slow down at all, something will go terribly wrong. It's worth trying to identify the 'terrorist' who planted that particular device in our lives.

People often remark in astonishment at the passing of time, 'Is it really only a year since...?' This is usually an indication that we have rushed through time at high speed. It may also be symptomatic that we are living life at a more superficial level. On the other hand, the person who has been grieving for a year will seldom say, 'I can't believe it's only a year since he died.' They are more likely to say, 'It has been the longest year of my life.' Grief is one of the most acute forms of emotional pain, and the pain actually forces us to slow down, and often to live more deeply. We are more in tune with our feelings, more vulnerable, more intolerant of the superficial and the cynical, more aware of the spiritual, more open to touching heaven. Paradoxically, it can be a very rich time.

Tragedies and sorrows can force us to pause, but we can also choose to pause and take stock. I make it a regular part of my discipline to take one Quiet Day every month, and one three-day retreat every year. These are always special days. They are days for slowing down. I will not allow myself to set tasks: it is not an achievement-oriented time. These are days for being, for growing, for listening more deeply, for trying to see if there's a shrub I've rushed past that is actually aflame with the angels of God. I need to open new windows of the soul, or re-open ones that have closed. These are moments of returning to God.

We may not all have the luxury of taking a day out per month, or several days off for a retreat (though we often have more choice in these things than we like to think), but we can still find little moments of quiet and withdrawal where we can deliberately become more attuned to God. The idea is not to put this kind of openness into a compartment; it is to change me so that I become more open in my everyday life.

LISTENING TO GOD

Dietrich Bonhoeffer was very clear about the need to listen to God. To his community, he wrote:

The one who can no longer listen to his brother or sister will soon be no longer listening to God either; they will be doing nothing but prattle in the presence of God too. This is the beginning of the death of the spiritual life and in the end there is nothing left but spiritual chatter and clerical condescension arrayed in pious words.[29]

Well, hands up those who have not prattled in the presence of God! I would think most of us have been guilty of it. This is the weakness of making our prayers in a rather surface-level way, automatically, coldly, and with no sense of being in an intimate relationship that is about conversation—speaking and listening. If we speak to God using formal prayers, it is all too easy to rattle off the words with our minds on something completely different. If we enjoy extemporary prayer, then we can become afflicted with a kind of nervous verbal incontinence.

Spiritual chatter is a serious Christian disease, and I think, in all honesty, we prattle with God for similar reasons that we prattle on with others. It can be a sort of defence mechanism. If we stop, become quiet and listen, we become vulnerable. It is clearly 'safer' to speak to God than to listen to him. You never know what he might say. Certainly in the Bible there are many instances of God saying rather uncomfortable things to people, and setting them fairly demanding tasks, as we have seen with Moses. When Mary was visited by Gabriel she was admirable in her ability to say little (Luke 1:26–38). Given the nature of what she was being told, she might well have tried to defend herself by asking many questions and giving several objections to the request. We can use speech as a defence mechanism.

I have a disturbing recurring dream. In it I am a guest speaker, giving a talk to a group of people. I become aware that what I am saying is undiluted rubbish. It is boring, irrelevant and disjointed, but I am carrying on because I dare not stop. If I stop, I will no longer be authentic. In the dream, people start to drift away, but I still carry on. I prefer talking rubbish to experiencing the hollow-ness of my words being exposed. The Franciscan hermit and writer Brother Ramon used to say that some people have a habit of going on talking long after there is nothing more to be said. This is me in my dream. In normal waking life, I am actually very conscious of audience reaction, and the moment I sense people looking bored, I start to bring my talk to a close. (I know, someone's reading this and thinking, 'So that's why you never speak for more than three minutes.')

The dream is my warning mechanism, alerting me to that part of me that can go on and on. At the same time, the dream indicates that part of me is frightened of being found fraudulent, speaking about something I know nothing about, because I have not stopped to listen. My dream is therefore an encouragement to listen, to grow wiser, to go deeper. Bonhoeffer sees a link between prattling on to people and prattling on in the presence of God, and he says that the penalty for this prattling is spiritual condescension—that terrible Christian disease that looks down on others and assumes they have nothing of relevance to say to us and we therefore have nothing to learn from them. Any fellow human we meet is worthy of our attention, and could be a messenger of God. Any meeting is full of great potential.

Bonhoeffer makes the important point that failure to listen to others inevitably means that I will be poor at listening to God. I am very sceptical when I meet someone who is supposed to have a prophetic gift, if I find him or her to be someone who shows no interest or ability in listening to me. It may be that they are actually quite good at listening, but they choose to listen to God, not me. I can understand that. God is rather more important than me! In fact, you could argue, once you have got the hang of listening to God, why bother listening to mere humans?

There is a problem with this attitude. Does Jesus ever give the impression that he is more interested in listening to his Father than to his fellow humans? I see no evidence of that in the Gospels. Clearly there were occasions where he was listening to both (for example, his conversation with the Samaritan woman in John 4, where he listens to her, but his prophetic insight suggests that he is listening to his Father at the same time). Even so, there are no stories of Jesus listening to someone and then breaking in to say, 'Excuse me, I've got a call coming in from Someone rather more important.' Jesus demonstrates perfectly integrated listening. He listens to his Father while he listens to others.

Jesus tells us that he does what he sees his Father doing (John 5:19). His relationship with his Father is not one of irregular divine phone calls. He and his Father are constant companions, and this is the model for us. Of course, there will be times when we will need to go to our equivalent of the quiet hills, and give focused attention to our Lord, but for much of our lives it will be a question of listening to God in the middle of our normal everyday lives. There is much pressure on us to live compartmentally: we have our Quiet

Time in the morning when we do our praying. We then go off to work where we do our working. We come home and have our family responsibilities. Perhaps we go to a home group and revisit the Christian department. We come home and say a prayer before going to bed and say goodnight to God before we go to sleep.

Such compartmentalism denies us the opportunities to see that 'lit field', that 'burning bush' that can occur in our everyday lives. As we have noted, we can become aware of the presence of heaven at any moment of our lives, as my father discovered when he was in his earthly childhood garden. These moments become wonderful opportunities for hearing God's voice, but they do not depend on a mystical experience. The mystical experience simply serves to remind us of the reality that God's heaven does break into our normal everyday life. I am all too aware that I get very absorbed in my work, but from time to time I like simply to pause and listen and seek to hear the Lord speaking to me. Quite often I hear something very simple that nourishes me, comforts me, challenges me, guides me—whatever I might need at that particular time.

Despite the materialism of our Western world, our longing for paradise will never be eliminated. Humans cannot live on the bread of this world alone. We all need the bread of heaven as we journey as pilgrims through an often barren land. God has put an amazing ability in our hearts to become conscious of the things of heaven. He has created windows in our souls that can open to see new views that can transform our lives. Like Moses, at any moment we may discover the extraordinary in the ordinary. Is this not one of the gifts that Christian people can offer to our world? We can be those who show that there is another world, not a million miles from this one. There is a kingdom of heaven that touches every part of this fragile earth. Everything in this earth can be touched by God to speak of things eternal. Part of our calling is to listen to others in such a way as to help them discover their own longings to touch heaven.

THE SPEAKER (6)

'I am telling them that you are a big speaker in England. An authority on AIDS. Very well known.'

Nkani was explaining to the Speaker what he was saying to the women. They were meeting in a rural school classroom after a two-hour drive along a very rough track. There were supposed to be twelve women here, but only nine had arrived. Though the room had windows, it felt rather dark and too warm, with flies buzzing around the windows.

They were sitting on children's chairs at children's tables. The Speaker felt utterly foolish, not for the first time. He was still borrowing Nkani's clothes, and today he was wearing a rather vivid purple shirt. He was perched on a little chair, trying to converse with nine women he had never met, none of whom spoke English. The size of the chair meant that his knees were higher than his bottom. On his uneven lap he balanced his leather briefcase, which was full of notes. He was expecting to read out some statistics on AIDS, although as the meeting went on he began to feel that very little in his briefcase would be of relevance. Why had he allowed himself to be hoodwinked into coming? He needed to be in a place where his skills could be used.

'These ladies care for the dying,' said Nkani. 'They work very hard. They go to their homes every day. They have been trained with some basic nursing skills. They listen to the person who is dying, and they listen to the family. It is a great burden, but these ladies here know Jesus, and he helps them.'

The Speaker felt sceptical but was polite enough not to question their faith. 'I imagine you need a bit of faith in this kind of situation,' he said. He was really speaking to Nkani, but Nkani translated it to the women. One of the younger ones answered. She had a chubby face that lit up every time she smiled, which was often. There was a serenity about her that was quite beguiling. When she spoke, she looked as if she was reciting poetry. She rolled her eyes and nodded her head. The Speaker was quite fascinated as he watched her and wondered if she was hearing music in her mind as she spoke. Then her smiles became less frequent, and were slowly replaced by a quivering mouth. She began sniffing and wiping the back of her hand over her eyes. Yet the smiles still kept breaking through the tears.

The Speaker assumed that she was relating another episode of this wretched AIDS epidemic, and was probably using her faith to try and find some good in it all. He imagined that she was complaining about the terrible consequences of AIDS and lamenting the poor health care in the community. It's what he would have been talking about, after all. He was actually getting very uncomfortable, and felt relieved when she finally ended her lilting narration.

Much to the surprise of the group, he didn't allow Nkani to translate, but instead said, 'Tell this lady that there are some important recent developments with the anti-retroviral drugs, and I have a meeting in London soon at which we will be discussing how we can make these available to folks like yourselves. It shouldn't be long before we can help you.'

Nkani looked slightly awkward, then nodded and translated for the women. There was a long pause in which no one said anything. Nkani coughed and said, very politely, 'Um, would you like to hear Sarah's story? I don't think I have translated it for you yet.'

The Speaker didn't really want to hear it. More than anything, he wanted to get his own clothes on and board a plane and go home. He was feeling hot, and the seat was uncomfortable, but he knew he had no choice. He did not want to hurt these women.

'Yes,' he said, and put his briefcase on the floor and looked at the red-eyed Sarah, who gave him a gentle smile before she looked at Nkani to give the translation.

'Sarah was asked to care for a little seven-year-old girl who was dying,' began Nkani. 'The little girl's parents and brother had died and she was the last one left. She lived with her aunt, who was not kind, so she had been very unhappy. She had to give up school because she had no money. She felt angry and at times she wanted to die so she could be with her parents and brother.

'One day, about six weeks ago, although she was feeling very ill, she went for a short walk—down to the lakeside. It was muddy, but she was too weak to stand, so she sat in the mud. Suddenly, she felt as if there was a crowd of people around her. She looked up and saw nobody, but she knew she was surrounded by angels. She could not see them, but she heard them singing. She had never heard such singing. She told Sarah that it was the most beautiful sound she had ever heard.

'She presumed she was dying when she saw a dark-skinned man coming to her, walking across the lake. Though this was very strange, she didn't feel afraid—she felt full of joy. At first she thought it was her father, but it wasn't. She didn't know who he was, but she ran to the water's edge to meet him. She suddenly felt completely strong. He picked her up and said just one thing to her—"There is still time to play!"—and they did. They splashed each other on the lakeside and ran around and laughed and tumbled in the muddy shore. Then suddenly he was gone, and the singing stopped. At least it stopped "outside". It never stopped inside her head.

'She came back and told her aunt, who beat her because she was covered in mud. The aunt thought she was making up the story as an excuse, so the girl did not tell anyone else, until she told Sarah just a few days ago. She died yesterday, and Sarah was with her. Just before she left us, she saw someone in the room. Sarah could not see this person, but the girl said to him, "Is it time for us to play again?" and started to laugh. She died while she was laughing.'

Outside, a class had just finished and the yard filled with the sound of children. The women spontaneously started to sing in wonderful harmonies, and Nkani joined them with his deep, beautiful voice. The Speaker was silent and for a precious moment couldn't care less about his lost suitcase.

Chapter 7

TO HEAL THE EARTH

If only we had the ears to hear,
Then we would rest our heads on the soil
And understand how
To heal the earth.

As I mentioned earlier, every month I like to take one Quiet Day—
that is, a day away from work, when I can think, pray, plan and give
time to listening to God. At some point on these days, I like to go
out for a walk. As I live in Derby, I haven't far to drive before I find
attractive countryside, and one spring day I drove out to the town
of Matlock and walked in the surrounding hills. It had been a long,
wet winter, and I was enjoying the warm breeze and the views as
I walked. At one point, the track I was following suddenly turned
sharp right, and ahead of me was a fence with a notice on it giving
a stern warning that I was not to cross it. Just beyond the fence, the
ground fell away steeply, because this hill had been dug away for
many years and the rock beneath was being dynamited, bulldozed
and pulverized. I was on the edge of a quarry.

After the serenity of the walk, this felt like quite an intrusion. The
beautiful hill that I was climbing was being demolished, and noisy
machinery was slowly destroying it. As I stood on the edge of the
quarry, I had a curious sensation, almost as if I could hear the earth
speaking. What I felt it was asking was, 'Who asked me if I could
be treated like this?' For a few moments, I became very aware of the
earth beneath my feet, the good world that God has created, and I
endeavoured to listen to it.

Inevitably the common-sense and heresy-seeking parts of me became alarmed, and argued back: 'The earth has no voice—it can't speak to you. That's New Age thinking. Anyway, don't go criticizing quarrying. There are many quarries in this part of Derbyshire, and it is a very important local trade…', and on they went. I tried to silence the arguments. I spend so much of my life listening to 'reasonable' voices, so why shouldn't I be just a little mad sometimes—if indeed it was being mad? The point is that, for the first time in my life, I found myself listening to this good earth that God has given to us as a home.

The Bible actually does affirm the idea of creation communicating. Psalm 19:1–6 describes it beautifully:

> *The heavens are telling the glory of God;*
> *and the firmament proclaims his handiwork.*
> *Day to day pours forth speech,*
> *and night to night declares knowledge.*
> *There is no speech, nor are there words;*
> *their voice is not heard;*
> *yet their voice goes out through all the earth,*
> *and their words to the end of the world.*
> *In the heavens he has set a tent for the sun,*
> *which comes out like a bridegroom from his wedding canopy,*
> *and like a strong man runs its course with joy.*
> *Its rising is from the end of the heavens,*
> *and its circuit to the end of them;*
> *and nothing is hidden from its heat.*

The heavens and the firmament all proclaim the glory of God. Not a day goes by without them communicating. The earth is full of the glory of God. Gerard Manley Hopkins, the Victorian poet and priest, puts it like this in his poem, 'God's Grandeur':[30]

> *The world is charged with the grandeur of God.*
> *It will flame out, like shining from shook foil;*

> *It gathers to a greatness, like the ooze of oil*
> *Crushed.*

Having celebrated the earth's glory, Hopkins goes on to ask with sorrow:

> *Why do men then now not reck his rod?*
> *Generations have trod, have trod, have trod;*
> *And all is seared with trade; bleared, smeared with toil;*
> *And wears man's smudge and shares man's smell: the soil*
> *Is bare now, nor can foot feel, being shod.*

In the eruption of the Industrial Revolution, Hopkins is horrifed at the effect this is having on the earth, yet he ends the poem with a celebration of the healing work of the Holy Spirit. We can have hope:

> *Because the Holy Ghost over the bent*
> *World broods with warm breast and with ah! bright wings.*

The poem catches the paradox that we often face—a world so beautiful, so radiant, so evident with signs of the Holy Spirit, and yet one that has been so damaged by its human inhabitants. Unfortunately we quite often leave it at that. We shrug our shoulders and thank the Lord for Greenpeace and Friends of the Earth and settle back and listen no further. Because of the crisis facing our planet at this time, however, the Spirit-filled community needs to listen afresh to the earth, to its glory and its pain.

ECOTHERAPY

When I studied pastoral counselling at St John's College, we read Howard Clinebell's *Basic Types of Pastoral Counselling*.[31] At the time, Clinebell was Professor of Pastoral Counselling at the School of Theology at Claremont, California. His book provided very helpful counselling tools for the parish minister who was not intending to become a specialist counsellor, and I certainly found it helpful in my parish ministry. It was to be many years before I came across his writing again, and that was when I discovered an article by him in the magazine *Contact*. The article was entitled 'Greening pastoral care to reciprocally heal persons and the earth'. I discovered that it was more or less a summarized version of his very impressive book *Ecotherapy*. In both the article and the book, he argues for the urgent need to attend to our relationship with the earth, both for our healing and the earth's.

In the article, Clinebell tells how he came to integrate care for the earth into his understanding of pastoral counselling. He describes how, while he was teaching in South Korea, he was invited by three young Korean clergy to climb Kyexyong-San, the sacred mountain in the middle of the country. He writes:

As we hiked up the mountain through the June woods, we were serenaded by a laughing brook and strange bird songs on a gentle breeze. Multi-coloured wildflowers displayed their splendour. Later, hiking down by a different trail, we came upon a large sign over the path. My Korean hiking companions translated it for me: love nature as we love our children! My first thought was simply, 'Good advice for everyone who cares about children and the earth.' Further reflection made me aware that, in today's global ecojustice crisis, to care for our own children, or for the children of the human family, fully and effectively, we must do what the sign advises. We must do everything we can to help them inherit a healthy earth on which they have the best opportunity to live healthy lives.[32]

Clinebell reminds us of the stark fact that the human species now has the knowledge and ability to destroy our planet. Indeed, this could be achieved not only by the use of horrifying destructive weapons, but also by misusing our resources and neglecting to care for the planet. Although our God has built into his creation the most wonderful healing systems, our treatment of the planet is testing them severely.

The biosphere—that incredible, interdependent network of living things (including us)—may be developing the planetary equivalent of AIDS, as its self-healing systems become more and more compromised and crippled. Scientists have warned that the timeline for our species to change its geocidal ways is probably very short.[33]

In his brief article, Clinebell makes a strong argument for integrating care for the earth with pastoral care. The health of humans is very much tied up with the health of the planet we inhabit. After all, what is the point of seeking to heal people if, in fact, we are destroying their environment? Not only that, but a sick environment will cause its inhabitants to be sick. The problem is serious now, but it is likely to be critical for our children. The Great Law of the Six Nations Iroquois Confederacy of Native Americans says, 'In our every deliberation, we must consider the impact of our decisions on the next seven generations.'[34] Such wisdom does not seem to be found among the leaders of the Western world.

In his book *Ecotherapy*, Clinebell develops all this further, making for a fascinating read. The part that moves me most is a reflective exercise that he sets the reader. In summary, he invites you to relax and then form a mental picture of the most beautiful place you have visited on earth. Having enjoyed this experience for a time, he then leads you on to imagine that it is 30 years in the future. You are still in the same place, but the destructive forces on the environment have continued unabated. Pollution has increased, and population growth has soared. He invites you to look around your beautiful place, to see how it has been affected, and listen to your feelings.

He then invites you to shift your mental gears. You are still 30 years in the future, you are still in your beautiful place, but this time the world community has been working hard over those last 30 years to protect the earth. The air is purer, the sea is cleaner, the ozone layer is being renewed, the poor of the earth are being cared for and so on. As you enjoy this experience, he asks you to imagine that a young child of about eight years old approaches you. She comes up to you and asks questions:

'What was it like back then? Were there really bombs so big that they could blow up the whole world? Was there really pollution that poisoned the air and water so people and animals were getting sick? Is it true that there were millions of children like me who were poor and hungry and sick, because governments were spending so much on things to kill people? Wasn't it scary then? What did you do to get through such a scary and discouraging time? How did you keep feeling hope so you could help make the world like it is today? What did you do to help give us children our beautiful, peaceful world?' The little girl spontaneously flings her arms around your neck and gives you a hug of gratitude. You feel her tears of joy as she whispers with deep feeling, 'Thank you! Thank you! Thank you!'[35]

REGARDLESS OF TOMORROW

This fantasy journey is simple to do on your own, and I commend it. Be warned, though, that it is immensely disturbing, for it makes us aware of our failure to care for the earth and our selfish lack of concern for future generations. The whole ethos of Western culture is concern for the now, not concern for the future. Returning to David Runcorn:

My parents were born, educated and socialized into a world that expected them to become responsible producers contributing to the good of the whole. Whether or not religion was explicit in this vision, the words 'duty' and 'vocation' were understood and approved. They were taught the importance of saving. Thrift was a virtue. There was a belief that things were worth waiting for, that tomorrow was important and was shaped by the values and sacrifices of today.

By contrast, my children are growing up in a world that requires them to be consumers. The central value of our society has moved from progress to choice. The consumer economy is a spending culture. The priority is today, not tomorrow. There is little incentive to save. We live in the present regardless of tomorrow.[36]

This tendency to live in the present, regardless of tomorrow, has dreadful consequences for our world. In the USA in 2000, the presidential election between Al Gore and George W. Bush was tightly fought. Each candidate campaigned for different issues, and most Christians voted, as so often, for Bush, the Republican. George Bush was reckoned the committed Christian, and therefore deserved to be voted into office to safeguard Christian values. Only months after getting into office, however, George Bush refused to support the Kyoto Protocol (the 1997 United Nations framework convention on climate change)—an action that many believe has potentially calamitous consequences for our planet.

Al Gore, on the other hand, was the Democrat who was not viewed as a 'Bible-believing Christian', although he studied for a time at divinity school before turning to law. He has long had a deep commitment to ecology and in 1993 wrote a much-acclaimed book called *Earth in the Balance: Ecology and the Human Spirit*. In this work he states:

Whether we believe that our dominion [over the earth] derives from God or from our own ambition, there is little doubt that the way we currently relate to the earth's natural systems is wildly inappropriate. But in order to change, we have to address some fundamental questions about our purpose in life, our capacity to direct the powerful inner forces that have created the crisis, and who we are... These questions are not for the mind or the body, but the spirit.

He shrewdly concludes this particular section of his argument with the words, 'Once again we might dare to exercise godlike powers unaccompanied by godlike wisdom.'[37]

I can't help feeling disturbed by the fact that the present incumbent of the White House seems to have little regard for the state of our planet, and haunted by the thought that we might have had a President who would have made the most powerful nation on earth a world leader in something that is really important—namely, care for this precious world of ours. It is also disturbing that huge numbers of Christians did not rate care for the planet a higher priority.

As you read this, you may be feeling moved, or you may be thinking, 'Here goes another eco-bore, writing out of ignorance. He clearly has no grasp of the complexities of the situation. What does he know anyway? I'll skip over all this eco-political stuff to something more interesting...'. I base this supposition on some experience! Having given several talks over recent years that have included references to caring for our world, I am sorry to say that Christians by and large don't seem to light up at the subject. They quite like loving nature, and listening to God in the countryside and that sort of thing, but radical and political action towards a more holy and just treatment of our planet doesn't really seem to matter to them.

Why is this? Perhaps it is because we are more influenced by the culture of our age than we like to think. The pressure to enjoy instant satisfaction rather than save for the future has gone deep into our psyche. Caring for the planet gives no immediate reward. If we spend our time in, say, evangelism, then we might be rewarded from time to time by seeing people come to faith. If we give ourselves to healing ministry, then we have the reward of thanks from grateful people, and even enjoying the excitement of healing taking place. Caring for the earth, on the other hand, brings no immediate rewards. It requires people who are able to have long-term vision.

If we will listen to the earth, then not only will we start to take action to help find healing for our world, but we will also find healing for that bit of us that has been taken in by the culture of the day—the desire for instant gratification. This ancient earth that God has entrusted to our care actually has a very important message for us. Its very age speaks to us about the value of time, and the need to care for our future generations. Maybe it could even instil in our souls that Native American belief that the decisions we make should bear in mind the next seven generations.

I am trying to develop a listening attitude to this world of ours. There are many ways of doing this. You don't have to go out to the countryside, though many will find that they are more alert to the earth in rural surroundings. Study the complexities of a lilac, feel the texture of the bark of an old oak tree, or spend time on a clear night looking at the moon, and listen to what they are telling you about the planet we live on. Walk down a busy road during rush hour, deliberately become aware of the exhaust fumes and, again, listen to what this is saying to you about how we are using the resources of our planet. I did this not so long ago, and found myself penning these few lines:

'Disgusting,' I say
As my car radio reports the death of another rainforest.
And the sickly sulphur belches from my car exhaust
While I, with lungs full of self-righteousness
Exhale the fumes that form as clouds of wrath
Over the children of a poisoned earth.

THE FORGOTTEN COMMUNITIES

You can't divorce the earth from the people who live on it. How we treat the earth in our neighbourhood will affect others who live in another neighbourhood. Care for the earth is connected with care for the people of the earth. Listening to the earth will inevitably lead us to listen to the people who are affected by the state of the planet. We can listen to our Christian music CDs in our car and empty carbon monoxide into the atmosphere, blithely ignoring the fact that there is a bereaved young mum in Bangladesh who has lost her child in a terrible flood caused by global warming—until we start to listen, that is. When we dare to listen at this level, it becomes very uncomfortable.

Care for the earth will inevitably cause us to listen more deeply to how we care for the communities of people who currently dwell here. One of the hardest things for Westerners to appreciate is that how *we* live is actually a minority way of living. Somehow, seeing scenes of pot-bellied African children and South American shanty towns does not move us enough. We may feel sorry for a time, but we are soon back into our 'normal lives', somehow managing to pretend that there are not really so many living in poverty, and that most of those who do are accustomed to it and don't mind too much. We may feel we have enough to worry about, and enough stresses of our own to cope with. We don't want preachers and writers banging on about how we should be concerned for the Third World poor. Let's leave the concern to those excellent charities like World Vision, Christian Aid and Tearfund.

In a previous chapter, I referred to an article by Walter Hollenweger in which he criticizes colonial forms of evangelism. In the same article he writes of his experience at the famous Congress on Evangelism in Lausanne in the summer of 1974. The conference drew over 2000 participants from 150 countries and, at the start, it was made clear that the important thing was the winning of souls, not matters to do with social justice. Samual Escobar, then General Secretary of the Inter-Varsity Fellowship of Canada, began his paper on 'Evangelism' with a story by Clifford Christians. It was a story that changed the direction of the conference and, arguably, the direction of evangelicalism. The story goes:

Imagine that all the population of the world were condensed to the size of one village of 100 people. In this village 67 of those 100 people would be poor; the other 33 would be, in varying degrees, well off. Of the total population only seven would be North Americans. The other 93 people would watch the seven North Americans spend one-half of all the money, eat one-seventh of all the food, and use one-half of all the bathtubs. These seven would have ten times more doctors than the other 93. Meanwhile, the seven would continue to get more and more and the 93 less and less.[38]

That was 30 years ago. I fear that the figures are even more stark now. Although the story talks about the North Americans, we could add the UK in there, as, compared to the developing world, we also have a hugely disproportionate amount of resources.

Recently I watched the film *The Beach*, based on the novel by Alex Garland. A small group of young people discover a tropical island inhabited by a community who are trying to establish paradise on earth. At first the young people are delighted—it is a beautiful place, with brilliant white beaches and blazing sun all the time. It is only a matter of time, though, before they discover that putting a group of people together in a place of great natural beauty does not guarantee that they will behave beautifully. Furthermore, although the sea looks gorgeous, beneath the waves lurks the danger of sharks, and there is one rather gory scene when three members of the community are attacked by sharks. Two of them die, but one survives with severe injuries. His cries of pain are so disturbing to the others in the big community house that, after a few days, the leaders of the community order him to be moved into a little tent, away from the camp, with a supply of food and water. There he can scream without upsetting anyone else.

One faithful friend stays to care for him, but the rest return to their carefree lives. They have created a paradise with no room for pain—no room, in fact, for any shadows at all. It is a kind of parallel to what so often happens in our world. There is something in us that would like to put all the poor and the hurting a long way away from us, so we can get on with our lives. But the problem is that they won't go away.

This is a real problem if we become listeners. As listeners, we won't be able to ignore the cries of the earth and the suffering of our world. We won't be able to ignore the look of the wounded AIDS sufferer in their hospital bed. We won't be able to think about our grandchildren in a polluted world without feeling discomfort. When we listen, we enter into the life of the Spirit who enables us to hear in such a way that we are not overwhelmed. And the reason he can do this is because of that wonderful word—eschatology. As someone once said, 'Don't worry if you don't know what eschatology is. It's not the end of the world!' Well, actually, it means the end of this world and the creation of a new world.

The Christian life is something of a balancing act. Christians are people of both the cross and the resurrection. In Philippians 3:10–14, Paul tells us his ambition:

I want to know Christ and the power of his resurrection and the sharing of his sufferings by becoming like him in his death, if somehow I may attain the resurrection from the dead. Not that I have already obtained this or have already reached the goal; but I press on to make it my own, because Christ Jesus has made me his own. Beloved, I do not consider that I have made it my own; but this one thing I do: forgetting what lies behind and straining forward to what lies ahead, I press on towards the goal for the prize of the heavenly call of God in Christ Jesus.

Here Paul is juggling with cross and resurrection, with the now and the not yet. It is one of the wonderful features of the kingdom of God. Paul wants to know his Lord and Saviour fully. He wants to experience the amazing power of resurrection, but he also wants to share the sufferings of the cross. He has come to believe that in this life it is possible to do so. He's not there yet, but he's pressing on towards it, which is possible because he belongs to Christ who suffered, died and rose again. Paul can put the past behind him and strain on towards the heavenly call of God in Christ Jesus, and this call is to both cross and resurrection.

THE FUTURE HOME OF GOD

In terms of the theme of this chapter, what are the implications of all this? As we look at our planet and the state of our world, we have to be bifocal to some extent. We use the short-distance lens to see our suffering earth, and we can feel its pain because we are people filled with the Spirit. It was the Spirit who was there creating the world, it is the Spirit who breathes life into the earth, and it is the Spirit who groans in us as we respond to a broken creation (Romans 8). If people claim to be full of the Spirit, part of the evidence for this will be sensitivity to the sufferings of the earth and its peoples.

But it is not all pain—not by any means. We can also lift our eyes and use our long-distance vision. In Revelation 21:1–3, we read about the creation of a new heaven and a new earth. I appreciate that we are entering realms here that are very hard to fathom, but I personally hold to an understanding of this passage which is that one day, the blessed Trinity will be engaged in an extraordinary resurrection activity that will transform the heavens and the earth. Not only that, but, according to these opening verses of Revelation 21, the ultimate dwelling-place of God is not in some far-off heavenly place, but on the renewed earth. The completely mind-blowing news that comes out of the book of Revelation is that God, the creator of the entire universe, has chosen our little planet to be his home. But then, after all, he was quite at home once before in a dusty stable in an obscure corner of the Middle East.

This news makes our planet even more special. Yes, it is going to be remade in some way, although we don't know how. This world has a wonderful, eschatological role as the dwelling-place of God. If we really believe this, then here is another very good reason for preparing a place worthy of our God. Hoping for a future world should not make us forget about this present world. It inspires us to change our world and make it a place fit for the return of our glorious Lord. We have a bifocal vision that enables us to attend to the pains of this world while at the same time trusting in its ultimate restoration. It is not a question of one or the other—it is one *and* the other. This dimension of hope has to be part of our listening to the earth. If not, the pain would be too much for us.

Howard Clinebell's appeal is for us to engage in 'loving listening', a term used by the theologian Paul Tillich. He describes it thus:

This means listening with caring as well as understanding, listening responsively without judging. To make the vital, unique contributions needed to help resolve the ecological crisis, counsellors, therapists, teachers, parents, and health professionals must learn to practise a new dimension of listening—responsive and loving listening to the earth. Unless more and

*more of our species learn to listen with love and caring to the anguished
cries of our earth as well as its shouts of joy when it celebrates creativity, it
is doubtful that our planet will survive as a healthy place for unborn
generations to come.*[39]

Some years ago I wrote a book on Celtic Christianity[40] in which
I included a chapter on the creative arts. A musician from the USA,
John Doan, read the book and contacted me. He was visiting the
UK, so I met up with him and went to one of his concerts. He plays
the harp guitar, an unusual instrument, and at his concert he played
an evocative piece of music in memory of St Columba. Before
playing the piece, he told the story of how he came to compose it.

In 1997 he decided to visit the island of Iona. When he arrived,
he was surprised to discover that it was the 1400th anniversary of
the death of Columba, so he found himself in the abbey at a service
celebrating the saint's life and witness. At the end, everybody left
except John. He had felt very moved by the service and, as he was
the only one present in the abbey, he went up to the altar, lay down
in front of it, pressing his ear to the ground, and listened. In those
moments, he told us, he listened to the earth beneath him, and felt
that he sensed something of its ancient story, and something about
the life of Columba. He heard it as music, which he later gathered
into the piece that he played to us at the concert.

Some might dismiss this as 'crackpot'. Others might say that
it doesn't sound very biblical. As I listened to John, I felt that
something profoundly biblical had been going on. Day by day
the earth and the sky pour forth speech (Psalm 19:1–2). John, a
musician and poet, had that gift of listening to the music of the
earth, a music shaped and fashioned by history.

If we are to develop a truly listening heart, we need to learn how
to listen to this world that is our home. We may not literally rest our
heads on the ground in the way that John did, but we can find our
own ways of listening. As we do so, let's pray that the Spirit of God,
the giver of all life, will help us understand how to heal the earth.

THE SPEAKER (7)

'How much money do you have in your bank?' asked Nkani. The Speaker was taken aback by the personal nature of the question.

'I really don't know,' he replied untruthfully. He was always meticulous about his money, and he had checked his balance before he left so that he would know how much he had to withdraw. He made sure he was never overdrawn.

'Does it feel good to have a bank account?' asked Martha.

'Don't you have one?' asked the Speaker, somewhat surprised. Nkani laughed. 'No, people like us don't have enough money to have a bank account.'

'Will you have some more chicken?' asked Martha. She was a good cook, and the Speaker was enjoying his boiled chicken and rice. 'Thank you. This is very good,' he said, as Martha delicately placed another piece of meat on his plate.

Night was falling. 'It gets very dark here,' he said.

'Is it not dark in England at night?' asked Martha. She loved to know what England was like, and envied her husband's visit there.

'Oh yes, especially at this time of year. But I live in the city and we have streetlights. You don't have streetlights here,' and this time they all chuckled together. It was the first time that they had all laughed at the same time.

'We love the stars,' said Nkani. 'Mosha told me about his time in the city. He did not like the city. He was there in winter and stayed in the township—such a big township, he said. And they all had fires with so much smoke. Also there was a factory near. At night he could not see the stars. People say it is like that in the West. Is that true?'

'Yes, it can be true, I'm afraid. We call it smog—a mixture of smoke and fog.'

'There is much smoke in the world,' said Martha as she started to clear their plates. 'We have put many poisons in the air. Why do we do that?'

The Speaker felt a bit unsure of his ground. He did not like being unsure of his ground. He was comfortable being an expert. He wished he had some of those reports to hand that gave facts and figures about the environment.

'Is it true that the President of the USA does not care about poisoning our world?' asked Nkani.

'No, I'm sure that's not true. Where did you hear that?' The Speaker rather surprised himself with his vigorous defence of a president of whom he was none too fond.

'You see,' said Nkani, as he poured the Speaker a mug of sweet tea, 'we care very much for our world. Sometimes, in the springtime, I get up very early. I wake when it is still dark, and I walk towards the mountains. I watch the sun rise—he rises far out over the sea.' Nkani waved his long arm in the direction of the coast.

'And, as he rises, so the mountains come to life. They wake up after their night's rest. I watch the golden light, first on the very tips of the mountains, which are covered in snow. They start gold, then become silver as the sun rises. Then the light reaches the rocks and trees lower down the mountain. Then the valleys wake up, and I stand there and reach my hands up to heaven. I imagine that my feet are on earth and my hands are in heaven, and I am the one holding them together—little me!' Nkani laughed delightedly. 'They are so close, you see, even someone small like me can hold them together. They don't need to keep their distance. They get on very well.'

'We need heaven to be close,' said Martha. 'I think our world is sick. Like our people here who are so sick, our world too is sick. I can see it.'

'How do you see it?' asked the Speaker

'With the eyes of my heart,' answered Martha, as if that was all that was needed.

'I'm sorry—what does that mean?' The Speaker felt foolish asking, but he found he genuinely wanted to know.

'It's like this. I go out some days and I am feeding the chickens. It is a beautiful day, and very quiet. Then I hear in the distance a roar. It is soft at first, but it gets louder. It is in the sky, and I see a little dot with white smoke behind it. It is an aeroplane. It goes over my head and I look up at it. It is so high, but the noise is so loud. It is full of important people going to meetings a long way away. I think of where they might be going. I feel envious of them.

'Then the plane goes away towards the mountains, and the smoke that is behind it stays in the sky. It is not our smoke; it is their smoke, but it is over our land. And the eyes of my heart see all the planes in all the world, and they see all the smoke in all the skies, and I wonder. What happens when the sky can hold no more smoke?'

'Well there are strict controls, you know,' said the Speaker sounding like an expert, which he wasn't.

'No,' said Nkani. 'You see, they have meetings, but no one invites the earth. I am not sure what she is feeling, but Martha knows. She knows, but she cannot tell me.'

The Speaker felt mystified and wasn't sure if he should ask further.

'I cannot tell Nkani,' said Martha, 'because the feelings have no language. But I hear similar feelings at the funerals. That is why I am troubled.'

They finished their tea. The Speaker had quite taken to sweet tea.

'Come,' said Nkani. 'It is a new moon.'

The three friends went outside. The air was warm, and the final colours of the evening sky were fading in the west. The delicate new moon was appearing over the dark bulk of the mountains. Soon a festival of stars would fill the sky. For the first time in his life, the Speaker actually noticed the world that he inhabited.

'Why did nobody ever tell me it was so beautiful?' he asked to no one in particular. Nkani and Martha knew it was a question only he could answer in his own time.

Chapter 8

TO CATCH THE WHISPER

There are times when I stand on a seashore
In the face of a wild wind
When I believe I begin
To catch the whisper.

There is a Zen saying, 'Knock on the sky and listen to the sound.' A few years ago, the sky caught our attention. We saw a sight that is witnessed only every two and a half thousand years: a comet came near our planet. In the silent night sky it passed us by and many of us stood outside on fresh spring nights and watched its smooth passage, marvelling that we could actually see the bright light and its sparkling tail. For a few moments, the night sky that we so often take for granted reminded us of its wonders, and for a few sacred moments we felt small and humbled in the face of such mysterious greatness.

Michael Mayne describes how he viewed the phenomenon on a mountaintop in North Carolina:

I watched through field glasses the comet Hale-Bopp moving across a clear night sky, trailing its broad tail of gas. None who saw it will forget the sight, made all the more awesome by the knowledge that it was last seen in the time of Cleopatra and that it will not be seen again for 2,400 years. The backdrop was a sky speckled with a myriad of stars such as I had never seen before: not only the familiar groupings of the Plough and Cassiopeia, but thousands upon thousands of pinpricks of light as far as my bino-culared eyes could take me. What my brain told me, drawing deep on odd scraps of memory, was an unlikely truth: that the nearest fixed star was about 25 million million miles away; that six specks of dust on Waterloo station represent the extent to which space is populated with stars; that, even so, there are more stars in the galaxies than there are grains of sand on all the beaches in the world; and that this planet on which I stood was just one of them. What my eyes saw reduced me to silence: a silence born of awe at the unimaginable scale of creation.[41]

For most of us watching and listening, this appearance of the comet aroused a deep sense of wonder and reverence, but two friends of mine heard a more specific message. I have mentioned before that after leaving university, I lived in a Christian community that was led by John and Ros Harding. In the 1990s, John was vicar of St Martha's, Broxtowe, and his wife Ros was very actively engaged in work in the local community, particularly with the Zone youth project that she set up. They were both being used by God in remarkable ways to bring his healing to a broken community.

Then Ros developed headaches that became increasingly intense. Just as we were hearing news that the Hale-Bopp comet was becoming visible in our skies, Ros received the devastating news that the headaches were the effect of a fast-growing tumour deep in her brain. Though for a while they hoped that the tumour was curable, there came a dreadful day when John met with the consultant who told him that Ros would have only a few weeks to live. He drove back from this meeting to break the sad news to his children.

As he prepared to do this, he heard news of the approaching Hale-Bopp comet and, through it, felt God preparing him and the family. His sense was that before the blazing comet disappeared from the cold spring skies, the life of Ros would pass from her wounded mortal body. His sense was right because, as it turned out, Ros did not have weeks to live, but days, and on the Friday after Easter she died. Her funeral was held in Southwell Minster, which was filled with shocked family members and friends who came to remember Ros, support John and the family and look to God for his comfort.

One mourner had a strange experience that she later shared with John. During the service she quite suddenly had a clear impression in her mind of Ros. She saw her as young and vibrant and more alive than she had ever been in this world. With a look of delight and playfulness Ros said, 'He has shown me all the stars.' Quite what the nature of this revelation was, we will probably never know, but for John this was an image that carried deep comfort.

I tell this story because it is a typical story of both pain and hope. John experienced the deep and terrible pain of losing his much-loved wife. But a friend was listening, who heard and 'saw' an image of hope, an image that greatly sustained and strengthened John.

The story speaks to me of the paradox that so often faces us in these brittle lives we lead. On the one hand we have those moments of being overwhelmed with wonder at God's creation, such as witnessing a comet. Along with the psalmist we sing:

> *O Lord, our Sovereign,*
> *how majestic is your name in all the earth!*
> *You have set your glory above the heavens…*
> *When I look at your heavens, the work of your fingers,*
> *the moon and the stars that you have established;*
> *what are human beings that you are mindful of them,*
> *mortals that you care for them?*
>
> PSALM 8:1, 2–4

Then, at other moments, we have to face the frightening vulnerability of our mortal lives. At one moment we can look at the glory of this creation and sing our praises in awe and wonder, and then we are brought down to earth with news of a sorrow, a pain, a sickness, a disappointment and all the other experiences that weigh down our souls. It is not easy to listen to both pain and hope.

HEAVEN ON EARTH

For many people, this all becomes very hard when they meet a crisis. Many of us have been close to people who, when suddenly faced with a time of terrible pain, look up at the skies and ask what kind of a God it is who inflicts such horrors on those he has created. God has given us the capacity to hold these different perspectives together, however, and he has placed a community on earth who are able to hold together both the glory of this world, which speaks so eloquently of a more glorious heaven, and the sorrows of this world, which bring such darkness. That community consists of the followers of Jesus—the Church. This is the community that is so full of the Spirit that it is able to bring bits of heaven to a wounded earth. It is a community of people who are able to stand on a seashore and watch the pounding waves and glorify the God of power and love. Equally, they can turn their gaze on the troubles of the world, those overwhelmed with deep waters of every kind, and, in the power of the Spirit, minister the compassion of Jesus so that the wounded find comfort, strength and healing. They are citizens of heaven who have learned how to live on earth in such a way as to transform it.

That famous evangelistic verse of John 3:16 tells us that God so loved the world that he sent his Son, Jesus. God's missionary predisposition towards this world is one of love and engagement. There are many, however, who have looked at the work of the Church and assumed that God's predisposition towards humans is essentially judgment and withdrawal. He is the God of the great 'Thou shalt not', who, from a distance, looks disapprovingly on the things people enjoy and calls them 'sin', and punishes and teaches them lessons by inflicting pain and suffering.

One of the greatest needs of our time is for people to discover that God who is in heaven is also on earth, and his essential disposition towards us is not one of punishment, but of love—to love people into deeper, better, more whole lives. The problem for us is that God is committed to working incarnationally. He delivers his grace to humans *through* humans. He became human, and then entrusted his ministry to humans.

To be a member of his Church is an extraordinarily sobering and humbling calling. It is to grasp consciously the fact of that awareness that 'Christ has no body now on earth but yours' (Teresa of Avila). We are his hands, feet, lips and ears. We cannot live our Christianity unconnected to those who need healing and salvation. Remarkably, God cannot do it without us—that is a principle built into his world. He is committed to working with us. The Church is his primary (though not exclusive) agent for doing the work of his kingdom on earth.

We are seeing signs that Christian people are increasingly keen to engage with God's suffering world. Thankfully, throughout history there have always been those who have lived and witnessed incarnationally. Some have become well known, such as Mother Teresa, but the vast majority have been unnoticed and unheralded. While they have been working hard to bring the love and healing of Christ to a wounded world, other Christians have been less involved, preferring to 'privatize' and/or 'spiritualize' faith. There are those who feel that Christianity is a private matter—it's personal. It's not the kind of thing we talk about. Religion should remain a matter of personal opinion and faith.

Many years ago, I was working with a church whose organist was a fine musician and had a cheerful, warm personality. His religion, on the other hand, was private. As the church experienced charismatic renewal, he became more and more anxious. In the early 1980s, the 'sharing of the peace' started becoming commonplace during communion services. Our organist was outraged by this. I remember going to shake his hand during the peace at one communion service, and he put his head down, firmly held his hands together and would neither look at me nor offer his hand. I was relatively new in ministry in those days, and was rather taken aback.

Paradoxically, when I was doing my 'clergy-shaking-hands-at-the-door' after the service, he came up and shook me vigorously by the hand, apologizing for not doing so in church. He said he was convinced that it was totally inappropriate to exchange this gesture during 'formal worship'. Sadly, despite many conversations and pleadings, he never could accept that Christianity was a shared, rather than private, religion, and eventually he left the church and went to another where, for a time, he found sanctuary—until that church changed as well!

Those, like my organist friend, who want to keep their faith to themselves are not just hurting the church fellowship. They are also denying the wider community, which the church is there to serve, from receiving the healing good news of the kingdom of God, mediated through the warmth of fellow humans who have found Christ.

The Spirit of God is driving us out into the wildernesses of this world, as he drove our Lord out into the wilderness after his baptism. There is a Russian icon called 'The Descent of the Spirit', painted towards the end of the 15th century and from the Novgorod School.[42] In the icon, we see the Spirit being given to a group of disciples. The Spirit is depicted as a dove at the top of a room, in which are seated twelve disciples. It is apparent that each disciple is being individually gifted by the Spirit, but the way in which the group sits in a circle corresponds to the shape of the group in Rublev's well-known icon of the Trinity, depicted as the three visitors to Abraham gathered around a table. Rublev's icon shows that the Spirit does gift, but at the same time he creates community, which parallels the community of the holy Trinity. Paul emphasizes this in his well-known teaching about spiritual gifts in 1 Corinthians 12:1–12, where he keeps repeating how the gifts are 'for the common good'.

In the 'Descent of the Spirit' icon, the disciples are gathered around a character in the centre, who is enshrouded in darkness. He is 'Cosmos', the person in the world who has not yet heard the gospel of Christ. He is holding the scrolls of the good news, but that in itself will not free him. He needs the Spirit-filled community to release him from his darkness so that he may walk with them in the light. It is a profound image of the work of the Spirit. I love visiting churches where I find a community with open hearts, where the gifts of the Spirit are being used not just for the church congregation, but for the wider local community which has yet to hear the good news.

LISTENING TO THE COMMUNITY

When I worked for Anglican Renewal Ministries in the 1990s, one church that I particularly admired was the Anglican church in Conisborough, near Doncaster. The vicar was Ian Chisholm, who served a community that had been traumatized by the collapse of the coal industry in the area. He sensed that his first task was to be a bringer of hope, and to help the church become a living sign of hope.

The church building is brilliantly situated at the heart of the town and, at the beginning of his ministry, Ian spent much time praying there, listening to God, and listening to the people of the area. As he listened, he felt that the first task to tackle was repairing the church building and repainting it on the inside. So much in the community was broken down that he felt they needed to have something beautiful in the middle of it all. He set about raising funds to repair the church, install heating and clear the churchyard. This was the beginning of a wider renewal. During the 1980s and '90s the church grew fast, and became involved in many regeneration initiatives in the town.

When I visited the parish, Ian took me to nearly new shops, coffee shops and retraining schemes that were all being run by local church people. Each and every stage of the work was characterized by listening. They listened with the ears of God, and they also preached the word of God, and the church grew strong, becoming a vital source of the wider community's healing and recovery.

There are signs that some parts of society are beginning to see the Church as a place of compassion and healing. It may take two or three generations, but I believe that a time is coming when the Church's reputation will no longer be one of a distant, judgmental institution.

I once heard a fascinating talk by Martin Robinson of Bible Society, about his research into the Wesleyan revival of the 18th century. He had discovered that church attendance figures did not actually rise that much during the time of the Wesleys. About 50 years later, however, the attendance figures soared. His understanding of this was that, during the early years of the revival, existing churchgoers were being 'converted'. They abandoned their privatized view of faith and began to work for the reforming of society. From being passive spectators, they became engaged in Christian service. People such as William Wilberforce were a direct fruit of this renewal. As a result, society's perceptions of Christians and church gradually changed. The cultural environment was changing. As people felt loved and cared for, it became safe for them to come to church. Once they did start coming, there were plenty of fiery preachers to tell them the good news![43]

A few years ago, Phil Baggaley, a Derby-based songwriter, was working on a musical project called *Shipwrecks and Islands*. He wanted it to be a collection of songs and poems that would help Christians to respond to that disturbing parable of Jesus in Matthew 25 about the sheep and the goats, and about our call to visit the imprisoned and care for the sick and so on. Phil asked me to write something for the start of the project, using the image of us standing on the safety of our island but taking the risk to look out to sea and become aware of the needs of a wider world. Working together, Phil and I produced these lines:

Safe I stand on my island:
Secure, while warm summer breeze blows from inland meadows
and fragrance from well-rooted trees and plants assure me of peace.
From the shore of my island I look inland
and see the strong granite rock supporting the stones of my dwelling
not spacious, but secure
and all is familiar.

But if I turn my gaze toward the ocean, I see the wild waves;
I hear the power of the tides pounding the pebbles of my land.
I see storm-tossed crests and tempests
beating at bows of broken vessels.
I dread the sound of the mariners' cry
and fear to hear the sobbings of suffering souls.
I long to face the shaded shore,
to plant my feet into the safe soil.

And yet, have I not looked inland long enough?
Is the restless ocean stirring my slumbering soul?
Does the Spirit move on the face of this dark water
To awaken me from comfort's sleep? [44]

The words still challenge me. I like being secure. I like what's familiar, and yet I find that the Spirit has the habit of disturbing me, calling me to explore the perimeters of what is safe. As I do risk looking and listening, then things can get a bit disturbing. I begin to hear voices to which I am usually deaf.

Later in *Shipwrecks and Islands* there is a song called 'Light of all lights', with a refrain that runs:

> *Do you hear there's a whisper on the wild winds,*
> *A distant cry that is calling through the storm?*

We need to listen to those voices that can barely be heard above the noise of this world. There is a Zulu proverb that says, 'What the poor man says is not listened to.' The poor are those who feel pushed to the margins. They may be materially poor in a wealthy society; they may be emotionally poor in a society that is not kind to those deemed to be 'losers'; they may be spiritually poor because they have never heard that God is a God of love. It is the people on the margins who, more than any others, need to be heard. I sensed this in the call of God I heard on my visit to South Africa: 'Go not only to those who need you, but those who need you most.' This is one reason why Acorn has been developing its Priority Area Listening project, working with churches around the country to offer listening care in those parts of our communities that are particularly needy.

Some years ago, some Christians on Merseyside did a listening course. They lived in Halewood, a community suffering from high levels of unemployment. As they learned to listen, they became aware of the hurts in their community, and in response they set up a project called *Listening Ear*. In time they found some accommodation that provided an office and some 'listening rooms', and *Listening Ear* is now a highly respected resource in Halewood. Health professionals, social services and other caring agencies now regularly refer people there, and people come for 'listening time' throughout the week. There they find a safe place where they can tell their story, knowing that they won't be judged, interrupted, pestered with questions or even given advice. They are simply given the space in which to tell someone about what is going on in their lives. Further specific guidance is available, if people want it, but in the main they testify to feeling greatly empowered and helped by 'just' being listened to.

I asked Margaret, a leader of the project, how she knows that people have been helped by this apparently simple act. 'Oh, I know they have been,' she answered very definitely. 'I work at the desk in the office a lot, and I see people coming in hunched up and frowning or nervous. Then, after they have been listened to, I watch them walk out with their heads held up. They have changed.' Acorn's vision is to see this kind of care taken into as many broken places of our society as possible. Being listened to is a basic human right, and therefore it should be available to all.

In my work at Acorn, I visited some of the places that had asked for training to set up a Priority Area Listening project. Not so long ago, I took up an invitation from Father Michael Beasley, who leads an Anglican church in Abertillery, South Wales. I travelled with an Acorn colleague down the motorways, and eventually along the valley road leading to Abertillery. As we drove between the sweeping hills, I found myself remembering bits of Dylan Thomas' *Under Milk Wood*. As the play begins, we are called to listen with the words, 'Time passes. Listen... only you can hear the sounds of the houses sleeping in the streets in the slow deep salt and silent black, bandaged night...'.[45]

Dylan Thomas invites us to join the town in the darkness of night, and we realize that we are those who are given ears to listen and eyes to see things not normally audible or visible. I was arriving at Abertillery not in the 'black, bandaged night', but in daytime, and I was aware that part of my role was to listen and to see. I parked my shiny, fairly new car in the rundown two-storey car park, which had no security, broken lighting, and a nauseating smell of urine and stale kebabs. We then had a meeting with Michael, and he revealed that he had indeed lived as a listener in that community. He told us how, following the collapse of the coal and steel industries, this small town had one of the highest unemployment rates in Europe. After a couple of years of pastoral involvement in the community, he was beginning to see the 'mazes and colours and dismays and rainbows...' (to use Dylan Thomas' language).

Strangely enough, I was moved most when he drove us around the town and pointed out a working men's club and said, 'This is where Tom Jones first sang publicly. His career started here.' I wondered how many others here had nurtured hopes of discovering some hidden talent that could make them a fortune and free them from their economic plight. So many in our land feel trapped by forces beyond their control. At least, here in Abertillery, there is now a small team of people emerging who want to spend some time listening to the pain of those who do feel trapped. I have no doubt that when those people get the chance to tell their stories, articulate their hopes and express their fears in a safe place, they will find a sense of empowerment that will bring healing and renewal to their lives.

LISTENING, A GIFT FOR OUR TIME

The need for people to learn to listen is arguably greater now than at any other time in history. There is something about the pace of our lives that means this quality has been all but lost. So much of our culture militates against good listening. Our TV-orientated lives mean we don't have the evenings of relaxed chatter that would have filled the after-dinner hours of our great-grandparents. When people fail to find a listening ear again and again and again, the consequences can be extremely serious. Many testify to the fact that when they are not listened to, they feel angry. Anger, which can often become hatred, is responsible for some of the most terrible atrocities in our world.

One morning, I decided to check this out in the newspaper. I did not have to look far. On the front page was the photo of a young Middle-Eastern father. He was wearing glasses and had a broad smile on his bearded face. In his right arm he held his young daughter, and in his left his young son. Behind him was a children's mural, and I guessed that the photo was taken at the children's nursery. His wife, so the accompanying article said, was five months pregnant with their third child. The picture suggested a contented family man. The article read:

There is no trace of evil in the beaming face of the proud father balancing his two young children in his arms. Yet Raed Abdel Misk, a religious scholar, was identified yesterday as the suicide bomber who snuffed out the lives of Jewish infants barely old enough to walk. The murder of 20 people, including 5 children—the youngest 11 months old—and the wounding of 120 others, 40 of them children, is being dubbed the Massacre of the Children.[46]

This kindly looking family man had strapped five kilograms of explosives to his body, and included nails in the packaging so that maximum damage could be inflicted on the occupants of a local bus. Those trying to defend his actions said that he was fuelled by hatred of the Jewish occupiers of his land and by endless humiliations to his people.

There is no excuse for such appalling brutality, but somewhere down the line this man needed a listener—someone who could listen to his deep sense of hurt and injustice at what he saw happening to his people. Most likely, those who did try to listen to him were those of a similar violent nature who also needed somebody to seek out those layers of emotion beneath the bravado, the rhetoric and the religious arguments. And now, of course, there are 120 individuals, plus their families and friends and the relatives of the 20 dead, who feel similar depths of hatred and anger. Will there be people to listen to them, or will they too remain trapped in the cycle of revenge?

On a recent trip to South Africa, I met a refugee from the Congo. He had witnessed terrible atrocities against his family and his people, and his soul felt full of sickness. Many of his friends had responded to the hurt and injustice with violence. Rather than responding to violence with violence himself, however, he found a listener. It happened during a Christian Listening training workshop, which he joined in order to find out what this 'listening training' was all about. During one of the activities, where he and one other person gave time to listen to each other, he found a safe place to tell his painful story at last. He found it such a liberating experience that he was instantly 'converted' to listening. He is now a tutor himself, and plans to join the team taking Acorn's listening training to the wounded country of Rwanda.

The gift is so simple, yet so desperately needed not only in the wounded communities of Britain but in all the places of violence, hatred and hurt across the world. At the start of this book I mentioned that plea by Freddy from Burundi, 'Can you please allow me to start listening, and then help peace to come to my lovely country.' Freddy was due to return to Burundi very soon and, by the time this book is published, listening training will be underway in both Burundi and Rwanda. I have no doubt that God will raise up groups of listeners in those countries that will be instrumental in bringing the healing of Jesus Christ to those broken lands. May there be many Freddys in the years to come, who can catch the whisper of the Spirit calling them to become the ears of Christ in our world.

THE SPEAKER (8)

'That was a very good lecture,' said Nkani as he drove the Speaker away from the hospital in Mosha's car.

'Thank you, Nkani. People were very attentive. They didn't ask many questions, though.'

'No,' said Nkani thoughtfully, then added, 'You have learned much about AIDS in your work in London.'

'Yes,' said the Speaker with a sigh, and looked out at the dry fields. He was struggling. He had just delivered one of his standard talks to a small group of medical staff at the community hospital. At home he had mastered the art of giving a lecture without looking at the faces of those he was addressing. He knew he took pleasure in being an expert. He liked the way people made a fuss of him when he arrived for a meeting, and the praise he received before and after his talks. He knew more about this disease than most people, and felt he was being useful sharing it. Out here, though, his knowledge didn't seem so valuable. Somehow, when he gave his talk, it sounded more hollow, more irrelevant. He put it down to the fact that it was probably over their heads—he had pitched it too high academically.

'What did you think of our hospital?' Nkani asked. He had to raise his voice as the car windows were open and they were travelling faster now.

'I didn't think it was very clean,' said the Speaker, and then felt bad that his first comment was critical. He glanced momentarily at Nkani and saw a little frown cross his face. 'But the staff are very committed,' he added quickly.

'They have a difficult job,' said Nkani.

'They certainly do. What keeps them going, Nkani? They see so much suffering and death.'

'What keeps *you* going?' asked Nkani quite innocently. 'You have given your life to this disease. It must trouble you, doesn't it?' The question took the Speaker aback. Nkani's comments felt uncomfortable. Why? He needed to give Nkani an answer, but couldn't find anything to say.

The vehicle was slowing down, and Nkani pulled over and parked just off the road.

'Why are we stopping?' asked the Speaker.

'I wanted you to see one of the most beautiful views in Africa.'

The Speaker clambered out of the car. His black leather shoes were now very dirty, so he no longer worried about where he put them. He was surprised at how relaxed he had become about his suitcase never turning up. The village people were now supplying him with shirts that really fitted quite adequately.

The land before them was essentially flat, but in the distance they saw it gently rising to greet the mountains, which were the same kind of blue as the sky, only in deeper shades. Not far from where they stood was a lake, and he could hear the chatter of children by it. He thought of Sarah's story of the little girl and the strange visitor. Around the lake, the land was green, apart from a field that had been recently ploughed. The earth looked very red against the surrounding grass.

Nkani was shielding his eyes with his hand because of the glare of the afternoon sun. The Speaker wondered how Nkani viewed the scene. 'What do you see, Nkani?' he asked.

'I see a beautiful land that has been home for me, my family and my ancestors. It is a good and kind land. Its rich soil feeds us. The mountains provide water for us. When we mix the earth with the water, we have good material for the walls of our houses. Years ago there was war here, and for many years black people have not been treated well, but we have moved on from that. The land is good and peaceful now, but I see shadows.

'That house there—a 14-year-old orphan girl looks after her younger brothers and sisters; in that house over there a lady has lost her husband and three sons; in that house—just beyond those trees there—a young wife is dying; and that house—over there by those rocks, you can just see it—that was Mosha's house. Everywhere I look there are signs of the disease. It is like the valley of the shadow of death.'

Nkani turned to the Speaker. 'This is what I needed you to see. This is why you had to come,' he said, and turned to gaze again at the little house that had been Mosha's.

In weeks to come, the Speaker would try to explain these moments, but would never find the words to describe them. He knew they were moments when things changed—when *he* changed. He knew that the talk he had just given was the last of its type. From now on they would be different—very different.

He bent down on the dusty earth as a noisy van rumbled past, and undid his dusty shoes with his dusty hands.

'Why do you remove your shoes?' asked Nkani, genuinely puzzled.

'Yea, though I walk through the valley of the shadow of death, thou art with me,' said the Speaker, surprising both Nkani and himself by quoting scripture. 'Isn't this what people did, when they stood in a holy place? He is with us—here in the valley of shadows.'

Nkani blinked a bit, and then crouched down and took his shoes off too, and both men stood in the dust in their socks, surveying the valley in front of them.

'Is it getting to you?' asked Nkani after several minutes of silence.

'Yes, Nkani, it is.'

'How does it feel?'

'Sad. I've not really felt this before. I know it sounds strange, but I suppose that's just the way I've been. Sadness was something I avoided.'

'If you've not known sad, then you probably haven't known happy either,' said Nkani. He turned back to the Speaker and his face was wearing one of the broadest smiles the Speaker had ever witnessed.

'Do you know, Nkani, the way you people face dying is actually helping me to know how to face living. I'm not sure I've actually lived before.'

Nkani chuckled. 'No, not if you were an expert!' he said, and laughed louder and slapped the Speaker hard on the back. The Speaker heard himself laugh—he had never laughed like that before. He wasn't organizing or controlling the laughter; it simply carried him along.

'I'll have to ask Martha to wash my socks,' said the Speaker.

'*My* socks,' said Nkani, and erupted in laughter again.

Later, back in the car, the Speaker asked, 'What *does* keep them going in the hospital there?'

'You discovered that just now,' said Nkani, and the Speaker smiled and watched the sun drop behind the mountains.

Chapter 9

TO DREAM OF
BETTER THINGS

Too often I reduce my world
to what is known and safe;
The time has now come
To dream of better things.

A few months after deciding to write this book, I went to Lindisfarne for a retreat. I have already mentioned that this is a special place for me, a place of insight, of thinking clearly, of gaining new perspectives and opening to new ideas. So off I went, determined to start work on this book. I did start on the book, but I was also in for a surprise.

I had arranged to stay in the home of Ray Simpson, who was heading off the island to some meetings in the south of England. Happily, I arrived just in time for us to have an hour together before he left. As we talked, we discussed a book that Ray was working on. As part of this book he had written up a 'dream' that he had had: he had sat at his computer and imagined what would happen if the church in Britain followed some of the principles of the early Celtic church. I found what he wrote out very inspiring and, as he was talking about it, I felt that it was in some way significant for my own retreat.

The following day, I decided to walk the circumference of the island to give space to thinking and praying about my work with Christian Listeners, and also about this book on listening. About halfway round the island, I found myself walking by the long white beach, not far from the causeway that links the island to the mainland at low tide. I rested on the edge of the sand dunes and looked out at the sea. It was a typical April day, with a breezy sky and a lively blue sea. My thoughts returned again to Ray's dream of a Celtic church, and I found myself wondering what a 'listening' church would really look like. It was a concept I had often considered, but I am not sure I had ever thought about it practically. As I pondered, I sensed a stirring of the Spirit; and then, rather more disturbingly, I felt God ask me if I would be prepared to lead such a church. As I was very settled with Acorn at the time, I put the disturbing question to the back of my mind.

I continued my walk, and when I got back to Ray's house I decided to write up my 'dream' of a listening church. I imagined that the dream would find a personal outworking a long way in the future. God clearly had other ideas, however, for not long after my return from Lindisfarne I was greeted by an unexpected turn of events that led to my closing my work with Acorn and beginning a new work with the Diocese of Derby.

As I prepared for the new job, the idea of the listening church would not leave me, and I knew I had to pursue it. As a result, I now find myself as the non-stipendiary vicar of St Paul's, a small church in Derby, and my sincere hope is that this will indeed be a listening church. A group of around ten of us have moved from a strong, lively church to join about the same number of regular worshippers at St Paul's. Together we are exploring what it means to be a church that makes listening one of its primary values. Our aim is to listen to God and to listen to the community that the church serves, and then to evolve a culture, life and witness that is shaped by what we hear. I suspect that, at times, this will feel dangerous and disturbing, and already we are finding that we are having to let go of some of our much-cherished ways of doing things.

About the time that this book is being published, we shall be going around the community with a questionnaire as a means of listening to the folk who live locally. The questionnaire will include these sorts of questions: 'How could the church help the community? If you came to church, what day of the week and what time would suit you best? If you came to church, what sort of music, songs and hymns would you like? What sort of subjects would you like to hear the preacher speaking about? And for how long?' The questionnaire will give us an opportunity to listen to the local people. Then we will gather their responses, look at the emerging themes, bring these themes before God and pray and listen to him.

The risk in all of this is that we may have to give up our preferred time of church service, style of worship and many other customs and preferences that are important to us. But if Jesus was willing to empty himself, leave the comfort of his heavenly home and take the form of a servant (Philippians 2:1–11), then I hope we will also be willing to leave our comforts for the sake of serving those whom God is calling into his kingdom.

At the time of writing, we have been part of this church for only a few weeks, but already I have seen one encouraging fruit of such listening. We were planning the carol service, and one member of the church said, 'I think God may be calling us to hold it outside, to show that we are a church that is willing to come out to the people, not expecting them always to come in to us.' There was a fairly long pause following this suggestion, and visions came to mind of a sad, damp-looking group of carollers sheltering under umbrellas, trying unsuccessfully to look like the band of the joyful and triumphant! But we quickly passed over such thoughts and decided to go for it. Amazingly, from nowhere it seemed, we assembled a brass band, a wonderful female singer for a couple of solos, a small choir, gazebo, coloured lights and sound system.

On the day, the wind calmed and the rain held off. A few minutes before the start of the service, only a few people were there. Within a few minutes of starting, however, a large crowd emerged, and by the end of the 40-minute service a crowd of nearly 200 had turned up, most of whom descended on the hall for a glass of mulled wine. I feel sure a miracle of multiplication took place that evening!

I learned much that night. One person listened to God and to the community, and heard what needed to be done. As a result, many people heard the good news of God who has come to this world to love and rescue us. Of course, we are not the first congregation to think of doing an open-air carol service outside the church, but the point is, we are learning that before we plan anything, we need to listen adventurously to the Lord and to the people we serve.

We are drawing near the end of this book. We have explored what it means for us to develop a heart that naturally listens. We have seen that it is deep in the heart of God that we should listen well to each other and to him. We have explored why listening is such a healing gift to our society at this time in history. We have found that listening well to those who are different from us can bring great rewards, not least the gift of wisdom. We have also thought about listening to our wounded planet, and opening our ears to those in the particularly troubled areas of our world. We have seen that listening takes us out of the margins of safety and, to take the example of the local church situation that I have described in this chapter, it opens us to think and dream of better ways of offering our ministry and mission. There is, of course, so much more that could be said about listening, but I can't help feeling that there is something wrong about writing a very long book on listening: it feels like talking for far too long, when I should be giving time to listening. Those who have ears—let them hear!

THE SPEAKER (9)

Nkani and the Speaker both looked at it. It didn't look in bad shape, considering how far it had travelled. It had gathered more labels and chalk marks, but other than that it looked much the same as it always looked.

'It has been to India, Nkani—imagine that!'

'But has it learned wisdom from the experience?' asked Nkani with a mischievous grin.

'I somehow doubt that very much,' said the Speaker. He knelt down on the airport floor, got out a key and unlocked his suitcase. There were all his belongings, neatly packed and somewhat compressed after being trapped in a case for over a week. The Speaker shut it again and didn't bother to lock it, but took it over to the checkout desk and watched it go off again on its conveyor belt. With luck, it might even get to London without doing a world tour on the way. To be honest, the Speaker no longer cared.

'There is much you have let go of while you have been with us,' said Nkani.

'Yes, indeed there is, Nkani.'

'How do you feel about going home?'

They had arrived at a coffee bar, and joined a small queue. The Speaker did not really know how to answer. How did he feel? He ordered two coffees and tried to think, to feel in his soul about his return.

'I have changed, Nkani,' he said, as he perched on a stool next to a high table. Nkani drew up a stool beside him, and poured two sachets of sugar into his coffee.

'Sugar?' he asked, winking. 'Sorry—go on, tell me.'

'When I left my home in London, I noticed how cold it was. It was difficult in those last days with Caroline—my wife, that is.' He had told Nkani very little about his domestic situation. He imagined

Nkani would disapprove. He imagined the whole world disapproved. 'It's not really a home, I suppose.'

'Are you going to divorce?' asked Nkani. The Speaker was no longer surprised by questions that he would once have considered far too direct and personal.

'No—we are just giving each other space.'

'And you have needed space, my friend,' said Nkani with a warm smile.

Yes, the Speaker did need space, but what he discovered in the space was not altogether comfortable. He did not like some of what he had discovered about himself. He was realizing that he was much more formal and cold than he wanted to be.

'I'm a stuffed shirt, Nkani,' he said, with a slight smile.

'Just remember whose shirt you are stuffed into!' said Nkani.

The Speaker's smile broadened. 'Do you know, Nkani, it feels very comfortable, and actually, while I am wearing this shirt, I don't feel like a stuffed shirt at all.'

'Then all you need to do is get some new shirts.'

'You may be right, Nkani.' He thought for a while, and Nkani gave him the time to think. 'To be honest, I can well understand why Caroline left me. It wasn't because there was anyone else—you know, another man or anything. I think I was slowly dying on the inside. She kept saying I wasn't the man she married. I had no fun any more. All I could think about was my job, and money and my powerful position.

'I completely denied that, of course, and argued back at her— shouted at her. I didn't get violent, Nkani, but I did get angry. I was angry because she was seeing what was happening in me, and I didn't like anyone seeing that.'

He paused, sipped his coffee and looked hard at a long queue of people at a nearby check-in desk. Nkani said nothing and sipped his coffee as well.

The Speaker came out of his apparent daze, and said, 'Perhaps...' But he had no way of finishing his sentence.

'Yes, perhaps,' said Nkani, and they were both happy to leave it at that.

'You will have to go through to Departures soon,' said Nkani, and a look of sorrow crossed his face. Then he added, 'While you were with us, I lost one of my dearest friends. But now I have a new friend. The Lord takes away, and the Lord gives.'

'Blessed be the name of the Lord,' said the Speaker, revealing not for the first time a knowledge of the scriptures.

'So, you will go back and speak at more meetings?' said Nkani.

'It depends,' said the Speaker.

'On what?'

'On whether I have enough wisdom, Nkani. You said I had come to bring light to the darkness of AIDS, but I haven't. In fact, despite all my research and expertise and PowerPoint slides, I never have. I can see that now. I have pretended to be a light, and you can't get more foolish than that.'

'But you have polished my mirror,' said Nkani, 'and I feel I will be a brighter light now.'

The Speaker felt puzzled. 'How on earth have I done that, Nkani?'

'Your cufflinks,' said Nkani, as if that answered everything.

'My cufflinks?' asked the Speaker, astonished. He felt his cuffs, and found they were undone. 'Where are my cufflinks?' he asked.

'Exactly!' said Nkani, and he pulled them out of his pocket and put them on the table next to the coffee cups.

The Speaker was not following this at all. 'You'll have to explain, Nkani.'

'When I first drove you from the airport a week ago, I noticed your cufflinks. I saw they were shiny gold and they were valuable. You are a wealthy man. You needed your suitcase and you wanted to go to a bank. But now, a week later, you don't even realize that you are not wearing your expensive cufflinks. You left them in our house.

'For the last two days you have not once mentioned the bank that you were so keen to visit, and when you saw your suitcase just now you could not care what happens to it. Don't you see, that is a big change.'

'Yes, I can see that is a big change—certainly for me. I have travelled a very long way.'

'Then, if you can travel so far by being in my simple home and village just for a week, there is hope. All we need is to make sure there are many homes and many villages where people can make long journeys.'

Nkani smiled a humble, slightly awkward smile, and the Speaker knew that, by comparison to this wisdom, all his knowledge was as useful as an unopened suitcase touring the airports of the world.

'It is time for you to go,' said Nkani as the noisy tannoy announcement intruded on their special moment.

'You will come to England again, won't you, Nkani?' said the Speaker as he got up from his stool.

'So I can be a big Speaker?' said Nkani with his huge African smile, and both laughed loudly, disturbing the coffee drinkers around them. They looked vaguely disapproving, which made the two friends laugh even more.

APPENDIX I

ELDAMA

On far off hills beams of pearl
illumine gentle African trees that shelter the earth
and reach to vast heavens.
Children chatter in their toyless play
while extravagant parrots swoop and blaze.
So eloquent the voice of God.

But in the valley a preacher
with aid of rasping voice and western amplifier
roars at a wilting crowd
that they must be saved and give their tithe
and once again the faithful fail to hear
the sacred songs of laughing love.

WRITTEN IN ELDAMA RAVINE, KENYA, DECEMBER 1995

APPENDIX 2

CHRISTIAN FOUNDATION

The Acorn Christian Foundation provides training in listening attitude and skills at various levels. All courses are led by trained tutors except for *Just Listen!* which is a short video/DVD-based training course for individuals or groups. Details of all courses can be found on Acorn's website or by contacting Whitehill Chase.

Acorn Christian Foundation
Whitehill Chase
High Street
Bordon
Hants
GU35 0AP

Tel: 01420 478121
Fax: 01420 478122
E-mail: info@acornchristian.org
Website: www.acornchristian.org

NOTES

1   Michael Mitton, *Wild Beasts and Angels* (Darton, Longman & Todd, 2000).
2   Nelson Mandela, *Long Walk to Freedom* (Abacus, 1994), p. 25.
3   The quotes from Margaret Wheatley are from an article entitled 'Listening as Healing', first published in *Shambhala Sun* in December 2001. The article can be found on her website at www.margaretwheatley.com.
4   Dietrich Bonhoeffer, *Life Together* (SCM Press, 1954), pp. 75–76.
5   *The Times*, Saturday 14 December, 2002.
6   You can contact the Bridge Pastoral Foundation at The Queen's College, Somerset Road, Edgbaston, Birmingham B15 2OH; e-mail info@bridgepastoral.org.uk.
7   Allan and Barbara Pease, *Why Men Don't Listen and Women Can't Read Maps* (Orion, 2001), p. 102.
8   Roy McCloughry, *Men and Masculinity* (Hodder & Stoughton, 1992).
9   From 'Listening and Responding', an article by Frank Lake that I received in 1978. It was then part of the Clinical Theology Association First Year Syllabus.
10 Bonhoeffer, *Life Together*, p. 75.
11 Jean Vanier's fuller writing on this subject can be found in his excellent book, *Community and Growth* (Darton, Longman & Todd, 1979).
12 Michael Mitton, *The Quick and the Dead* (Grove Books, 1987); Michael Mitton and Russ Parker, *Healing Death's Wounds* (Eagle, 2002).
13 Bonhoeffer, *Life Together*, p. 76.
14 *Journal of Pentecostal Studies* Issue 7, 1995.
15 *Journal of Pentecostal Studies* Issue 7, p. 116.
16 Bede, *Ecclesiastical History*, English translation (Penguin, 1955), p. 146.
17 Bede, *Ecclesiastical History*, p. 151.
18 Richard Foster, *Celebration of Discipline* (Hodder & Stoughton, 1980), p. 1.
19 Jean-Dominique Bauby, *The Diving-Bell and the Butterfly* (Fourth Estate, 1997), pp. 104f.
20 Bauby, *The Diving-Bell and the Butterfly*, p. 13.
21 Craig Bartholomew, *Reading Proverbs with Integrity* (Grove, 2001), p. 8.
22 F.C. Happold, *Mysticism: A Study and an Anthology* (Penguin, 1963), p. 129.
23 David Runcorn, *Choice, Desire and the Will of God* (SPCK, 2003), p. 66.
24 R.S. Thomas, 'The Bright Field' in *Later Poems* (Papermac, 1972), p. 81.
25 John Taylor, *The Go-between God* (SCM Press, 1972), p. 45.
26 Ken Gire, *Windows of the Soul* (Zondervan, 1996), p. 18.
27 Kathleen Raine, 'The Wilderness', *Collected Poems* (Allen & Unwin, 1981), p. 107.
28 Gire, *Windows of the Soul*, p. 91.
29 Bonhoeffer, *Life Together*, p. 75.

30 Gerard Manley Hopkins, 'God's Grandeur' in *Poems and Prose of Gerard Manley Hopkins* (Penguin, 1953), p. 27.
31 Howard Clinebell, *Basic Types of Pastoral Counselling* (Abingdon, 1966)
32 Clinebell in *Contact* 133, 2000, 1–2, p. 3.
33 Clinebell in *Contact*, p. 4.
34 Quoted in Clinebell, *Ecotherapy* (Fortress Press, 1996), p. 78.
35 Clinebell, *Ecotherapy*, p. 18.
36 Runcorn, *Choice, Desire and the Will of God*, p. 66.
37 Al Gore, *Earth in the Balance: Ecology and the Human Spirit* (Penguin, 1993). Quotes taken from pages 267, 238–39, 240.
38 Quoted in *Journal of Pentecostal Studies* Issue 7, p. 111.
39 Clinebell, *Ecotherapy*, p. 14.
40 Michael Mitton, *Restoring the Woven Cord* (Darton, Longman & Todd, 1995).
41 Michael Mayne, *Learning to Dance* (Darton, Longman & Todd, 2001), p. 46.
42 For more about this icon, see Henri Nouwen's *Behold the Beauty of the Lord* (Ave Maria Press, 1987), p. 59ff.
43 A lecture by Martin Robinson at the Charismatic Leaders' Conference, December 2001. Further details of Bible Society from www.biblesociety.org.uk.
44 P. Baggaley et al, *Shipwrecks and Islands* (Gold Records, 1999).
45 Dylan Thomas, *Under Milk Wood* (Dent, 1954), p. 3.
46 *The Times*, 21 August, 2003.